THE FRAGRANCE OF CHRIST

VOLUME I

FR. LOUKA SIDAROUS

STORIES OF ORDINARY PEOPLE
STRIVING FOR EXTRAORDINARY HOLINESS

ST MARY & MOSES ABBEY PRESS

The Fragrance of Christ: Volume I
By Fr. Louka Sidarous

Icons designed by: Fadi Mikhail

Translated, edited, and designed by:
St. Mary & St. Demiana Convent
330 Village Dr.
Dawsonville, GA 30534
convent.suscopts.org

Published by:
St. Mary & St. Moses Abbey Press
101 S Vista Dr, Sandia, TX 78383
stmabbeypress.com

10 9 8 7 6 5 4 3 2 1

CONTENTS

FOREWORD

Hegumen Fr. Louka Khalaf Sidarous, born Kamal Khalaf Sidarous on Friday, May 3, 1940, in Upper Egypt, exemplified true union with Christ throughout his life. He grew up in a pious family. His mother was known for her love of prayer and the word of God, and his father was known to be a wise and godly man.[1] Kamal carried this firm foundation into his service and career. After graduating in 1964 with a Bachelor of Science, he began working as a lecturer at the University of Alexandria.

It was then that Kamal found God calling him to a different path.

On March 17, 1967, His Holiness Pope Kyrillos VI ordained Kamal as a presbyter, giving him the name Fr. Louka. He was elevated to the priestly rank of Hegumen by His Holiness Pope Shenouda III in 1989.

Fr. Louka began his ministry at St. George Church in Sporting, Alexandria, alongside Hegumen Fr. Bishoy Kamel. Their incredible bond of spiritual friendship is evident throughout this book, where Fr. Louka frequently uses "we" to indicate when they served side-by-side. Fr. Louka's ministry later expanded to St. Mark Church in Los Angeles and

---

[1] For more insight on Fr. Louka's upbringing and childhood, read *The Personal Memoirs of Fr. Louka Sidarous*, published by St. George Church in Sporting, Alexandria.

continued with the establishment of St. Mercurius and St. Abraam Church in Torrance, California, in 1989.

Fr. Louka's journey was not without trials, however. In the early 1980s, amid political tensions, President Anwar Sadat of Egypt ordered the incarceration of numerous religious figures, including Fr. Louka, who was confined in Wadi El Natrun and El Marg prisons, along with several other clergy members. He endured seven months of imprisonment under the Sadat and Mubarak regimes. Despite the harsh conditions, he remained spiritually steadfast. He and his fellow prisoners conducted daily prayers and Bible studies and even celebrated Church feasts within the prison walls. Fr. Louka viewed his imprisonment as a period of spiritual growth. He believed that true freedom is found in Christ, as it is written, "if the Son makes you free, you shall be free indeed" (Jn 8:36). His reflections on this time, detailed in his work *Memoirs of My Imprisonment,* reveal that, despite the physical confinement, his spirit remained completely unbound, continually seeking communion with God.[2]

Fr. Louka Sidarous departed on the early morning of Wednesday, August 26, 2020, leaving behind an example of faith, humility, and love, and encouraging all his spiritual children to pursue the life of consecration and holiness he lived daily.

This English translation of *The Fragrance of Christ* allows a wider audience to access the inspiring accounts and spiritual insights that Fr. Louka recorded. He wrote these stories in simple words that are filled with the spirit of Scripture. Most

---

[2] More accounts of this time can be read in *I Rejoice in My Chains*, a collection of memoirs by formerly imprisoned bishops and priests.

of the verse references in this text were added during translation—highlighting how Fr. Louka effortlessly and naturally expressed himself with the Bible always on his lips. As you read this treasured six-volume work, may you be edified by these stories, which give us a glimpse into the lives of those who walked closely with Christ. Christ's love is made visible in His faithful followers who struggle and persevere against sin. When one returns to Christ, others return to Christ! We are all indeed called to sainthood and holiness, as we proclaim in the Holy Liturgy, "Holies for the holy!"

The holy men and women described in this book were ordinary people, yet they simply reflected our Lord's light and love in everything they did. May you also begin to reflect Christ in this manner, as St. Paul writes, "For we are to God the fragrance of Christ among those who are being saved and among those who are perishing" (2 Cor 2:15).

May the Lord bless this work for the glory of His name, for the edification of His Church, and for the encouragement of His flock—those who seek to pursue holiness even in the mundane, the normal, and the ordinary. Through the intercessions of St. Mary the Mother of God and St. Mark the Evangelist, and the prayers of His Holiness Pope Tawadros II, may this book serve as a source of spiritual growth for its readers.

His Eminence Metropolitan Youssef
Coptic Orthodox Diocese of the Southern United States
Abbot of St. Mary & St. Moses Abbey and St. Mary & St. Demiana Convent

PREFACE

*An Excerpt of a Sermon by the Reverend Hegumen
Fr. Louka Sidarous on "The Pleasing Aroma of Christ"*

The Gospel tells us that many Jews, indeed a great number, saw Lazarus and believed in Christ. This teaches us that if one of us repents of their sins, turns away from their past, and becomes a witness to Christ, they can inspire many others to come to Him. Do you see how we might fall short? If I don't live as a Christian, I fail to witness to Christ. That is a tremendous loss! Yet, through repentance, any one of us can witness to Him. People would then say, "Look at that! Their past was terrible. They were corrupted, but now look at how they've completely changed!" Such transformation leads others to rethink their life of sin, inspired by a repentant person who has received the grace of life in Christ. When someone truly lives in Christ, they become radiant and beautiful, and their actions naturally draw the attention of others.

The opposite is also true: if one of us is known by name as being alive but is spiritually dead—just as it is written in the book of Revelation, "you have a name that you are alive, but you are dead" [Rev 3:1]—it is a profound loss! Outwardly, they may appear alive in Christ, but inwardly, they are dead. That's why I urge each of us to examine ourselves deeply today; am I truly alive? Is Christ genuinely the source of my life? Has Christ resurrected me? Am I living in the fullness of life, in resurrection, in light, and in holiness—or not?

Mary was the disciple who worshiped at Jesus' feet throughout her life. She was silent, speaking little, sitting at Jesus' feet and listening to words of love from Scripture. What did she do? She brought an alabaster jar of very costly spikenard oil—the savings of her entire life—and poured it out on Christ. This fragrant oil, of very great value, is mentioned in the Gospel. And what happened when she poured it out? The house was filled with its beautiful fragrance! This is pure worship—offered from the heart with a sacred spiritual passion, poured out upon the body of Christ.

If we were to bring a bottle of this very costly oil and open it anywhere in the church, the entire church would be filled with its scent. This is worship! These are the beautiful souls who loved Christ from the depths of their hearts and with sacred passion. They are the ones who make the church fragrant. They are called the "fragrance of Christ." Those who live as saints spread this sweet aroma. We thank God that this fragrance, which fills the church, exists in every generation and in every place.

People may complain, saying, "We've become terrible! Look at what our homes have become—chaotic and disordered. Look at the arguments and the inappropriate words spoken. Look at people who come from who-knows-where, with no connection to Christianity." Say what you will, but even amidst all this, you will still find the beautiful fragrance of Christ. It could be in a man, or a lady, or a young boy, or an elderly woman, or someone very poor, or someone very wealthy—people from all walks of life.

I remember when I began writing about the saints I had met, I reviewed what I had written and realized they came from all kinds of backgrounds—some were very poor, others were very rich; some were highly educated, while others had no formal education. Yet, the fragrance of Christ remained. You'll find in every church, in every place, and in every family, someone who carries this beautiful fragrance.

Where does this come from? It comes from worship, from prayer, from sitting at the feet of our Savior. The world is worth nothing if we learn to sit at the foot of the cross and gaze at Him! This coming week [Passion Week] is filled with that. Where should we be? Let's sit in the church. Why? To sit under His feet, so that perhaps our hearts might be moved, and someone among us might gather others to Christ! This will fill the entire church, the whole house, with the fragrance of the oil.

INTRODUCTION

In the name of the Father, and of the Son, and of the Holy Spirit, one God. Amen.

Many people define the lives of the saints by detachment from the world and a physical distance from it. They perceive that the path of holiness or life with God, in its entirety, requires going far away to a monastery or to a cave. Some written works have unintentionally helped spread these ideas through their portrayals of the lives of the saintly fathers and monastics. These ideas are further established when servants of the word incorporate them in their sermons, commonly illustrating aspects of holiness using stories of the saintly desert fathers. Some even oversimplify their sermons, beginning them with phrases like "Once, there was a monk who was a saint," or "Once, there was a saint who was a monk," etc. As a result of these sermons, the attending laity begin to only imagine saints as monks worshiping in the wilderness.

Our heritage and teachings, both spoken and written, rarely acknowledge that the Church includes countless poor and wealthy laity, from all walks of life, in all generations, and of all ages, who are righteous witnesses to the Lord.

We do not wish to diminish the value of monasticism, the saintly characteristics of the monastic life, nor the sanctity of the fathers who forsook the world and trampled it underfoot because they loved Christ more than the world. Nor do we deny the contributions of our fathers, the saintly monks throughout the history of the Church—whether early Christian saints whose stories have reached the ends of the earth or the more contemporary saints. We would only like to emphasize that a saint in the Orthodox tradition is not defined as a worker of miracles, but, rather, as anyone who walks and struggles along the path of holiness.

The Church, since its beginning, has been supported by the Holy Spirit through the signs and miracles performed at the hands of the apostles. The Lord bore witness to the word of His grace, "these signs will follow those who believe" (Mk 16:17). The power to heal the sick, cast out demons, and perform miracles was given to spiritually gifted individuals within the Church through the divine support of the Holy Spirit.

The Church has always been characterized by holiness, and the faithful have always been called saints:

❖ "Paul, an apostle of Jesus Christ by the will of God, and Timothy our brother, To the saints and faithful brethren in Christ" (Col 1:1–2).

❖ "Paul and Timothy, bondservants of Jesus Christ, To all the saints in Christ Jesus" (Phil 1:1).

❖ "Paul, an apostle of Jesus Christ by the will of God, To the saints who are in Ephesus, and faithful in Christ Jesus" (Eph 1:1).

❖ "Paul, an apostle of Jesus Christ by the will of God, and Timothy our brother, To the church of God which is at Corinth, with all the saints" (2 Cor 1:1).

So, holiness does not consist in performing miracles, but in the Christian life that conforms, in its entirety, to the teachings of the Lord, thus exuding the sweet aroma of Christ naturally and sincerely. This is why we decided to share the stories of ordinary people, whom we have seen with our own eyes and lived with closely, whose holy lives were filled with the fragrance of Christ.

What we are presenting are examples of such lives. We have recorded their stories in simple words that reveal the depth and richness of their lives—the lives of those who lived by the Spirit according to the commandments of the Gospel.

We ask the Lord that this may be the beginning of a full record of ordinary people striving for extraordinary holiness.

Fr. Louka Sidarous

CHAPTER ONE

Amm Sadek

A mm Sadek Raphael lived in Cairo until 1960.[1] There, he was loved by many people, especially at the Church of the Blessed Virgin Mary in Rod El Farag, Shubra, where he prayed for many years. During the final days of his life, he lived near St. George Church in Sporting, Alexandria. He departed to the heavens in 1969 at the age of 68.

The life of this righteous man was characterized by simplicity, purity, and depth. In his youth, he did not join his peers in their diversions. His strong relationship with Christ was a source of purity and chastity for his mind, enabling him to retain the pure heart of a child even into his adult years.

Amm Sadek had, in his early days, decided in his heart to dedicate his entire life to holiness for the sake of Christ, who loved him and laid down His life for him. He had intended to

---

[1] *Amm* (عم) is an Arabic word meaning 'Uncle' that is also used as a term akin to 'Mr.' or 'Sir' when addressing an elder or someone of respect.

go to a monastery, but his older brother passed away suddenly at a young age, leaving a wife and young daughter behind. Faced with this responsibility, Amm Sadek decided to put his plans aside and wait until his sister-in-law remarried or found stability.

During this time, his mother, whom he deeply honored and loved, fell ill. In her final moments, she pleaded with him, saying, "Do not go to the monastery until you are sure of your sister-in-law's well-being."

He promised her, and she passed away that same day. So, Amm Sadek became the sole supporter for his brother's wife and her daughter. His sister-in-law received many marriage proposals, but, inspired by Amm Sadek's life of prayer, spiritual fulfillment through the Gospel, and detachment from the world, she chose not to marry again and instead dedicated her life fully to Christ.

And so it was. Amm Sadek continued to support her and raise his niece. He worked for the Ministry of Justice, where he gained the trust of his superiors and the love of his subordinates. Wherever this holy man went, people bore witness that he was truly a man of God. Indeed, he was the "salt of the earth" and the "light of the world" (Mt 5:13–14).

After retiring, he left Cairo, moved to Alexandria, and devoted all his time to his spiritual life. God's grace filled him so that he became a fountain of heavenly comfort and spiritual depth. Whenever he spoke, his words flowed like powerful currents of holy wisdom. All who heard him were deeply moved, experiencing joy, repentance, and an indescribable sense of spiritual renewal.

He once told me about a visit to a Christ-loving family in Cairo. That evening, they gathered in conversation, encouraging one another with words of grace. Time passed without them noticing until they were startled by the call of the milk vendor outside—the morning had come while they were still enraptured in spiritual joy! They prayed, and then Amm Sadek left for work.

It was a great comfort to his sister-in-law to find, near her home in Cairo, the Orphanage of the Virgin Mary, founded by the late Hegumen Fr. Dawood El-Maqary, a saintly man who was a dear friend of Amm Sadek's. She began dedicating herself to the children there, showering them with love and care.

One Saturday night during the Coptic month of Koiahk, Amm Sadek and his sister-in-law were singing praises in church as usual.[2] His sister-in-law was seen sitting with and embracing some children from the orphanage, resting them on her knees. With a simple, innocent heart, she whispered to Amm Sadek, "Oh Sadek, my brother! If only the Virgin would

---

[2] The Coptic calendar consists of 13 months: 12 months of 30 days each and a short thirteenth month of five or six days, depending on whether it is a leap year. The months are as follows: *Thoout, Paope, Hator, Koiahk, Tobe, Meshir, Paremhotep, Parmoute, Pashons, Paone, Epep, Mesore,* and *Nasi* (or *El-Nasi*). Fr. Louka occasionally references these months.

come now and gladden us with her presence as we keep vigil to celebrate her."

Before she finished her words, the Holy Virgin appeared to them in full form, walking in the sanctuary. Amm Sadek knelt on the floor as his sister-in-law joyfully hailed and praised the pure saint. Strangely, none of the other worshipers present, except for a few of the younger children, witnessed the apparition.

His Life in Alexandria

Amm Sadek fled from Cairo because he had become well-known there, and he preferred to live a secluded, quiet life away from everyone. When he came to Alexandria, he sought solitude and avoided interacting much with others.

He lived near St. George Church in Sporting and became acquainted with the late Hegumen Fr. Bishoy Kamel, who was just beginning his priesthood. When Fr. Bishoy would get tired during his ministry and need to rest, he would go to Amm Sadek's home. Together, they would find comfort in the abundant spiritual benefits of the word of God.

A few of the youth, particularly those living far from their hometowns, saw Amm Sadek as a teacher and a source of blessing. But he did not accept invitations to deliver sermons at the church or its meetings. He used to say, "God has appointed for the church: first apostles, second prophets, third teachers [1 Cor 12:28]. The Spirit did not choose me as a teacher, but I find comfort with my brethren who share the faith with me, and all that I receive from God, I freely give to everyone."

Liturgical Prayer

A sight that will remain etched in my memory forever is the image of Amm Sadek at church during the liturgy. I can truthfully say I have never seen anything else like it.

He would enter the church in utter piety and go to the side altar, where he would kneel with reverence. Then, he would enter the men's side of the sanctuary and worship towards the altar. He would stand there until the end of the liturgy, without a single movement, as if nailed to the ground.

The moment he entered the church and stood facing the altar, his eyes would become fountains of tears resembling Jeremiah's flowing waters (Jer 9:1). The entire congregation witnessed Amm Sadek's unceasing tears during every liturgy. Where did these tears come from, if not from a pure, compassionate heart filled with sensitive spiritual emotions and a keen awareness of the presence of Christ?

Self-Denial

During a conversation with the late Pope Kyrillos VI in 1967 inside the altar of St. Mark's Cathedral in Alexandria, the saintly pope asked me to bring him Amm Sadek. That same day, I went to Amm Sadek and told him that His Holiness wanted to see him.

Those words came upon him like a tempest, and he started weeping in a loud voice, saying, "May God forgive you! You should have kept me concealed until I passed away. What does the pope want from a lowly creature like me?"

I tried to calm him, reassuring him that it was simply a meeting, nothing more than an introduction or a greeting.

Finally, he said, "I will go and obey his word, but I will greet him and take his blessing among the people without revealing myself to him."

He then pleaded with Christ, through prayers and supplications, that the pope would not recognize him, for he knew that the Lord had granted Pope Kyrillos VI the gift of discerning hidden matters.

And so, God fulfilled his request. Amm Sadek kissed the pope's hand in the midst of the crowd, and the pope did not recognize him. Thus, this righteous person displayed an extraordinary humility and a poverty of spirit that is rarely witnessed in our present time.

Grace

The teachings of Amm Sadek were evident through his actions. His personal life and words were full of wisdom and spiritual depth. He always attributed this to the grace of God, denying himself as the doer or speaker. When he spoke, he would make the sign of the life-giving cross over his mouth and say, "Grace tells us . . ." before continuing. He often admitted that he considered himself first among the listeners and that he benefited from the word before teaching others about it.

Beyond Imagination

Once, in the beginning of my priesthood, I was praying the Holy Liturgy, and Amm Sadek had been, as usual, standing in the side sanctuary from the very beginning of the service. I gave the sermon and interpreted the Gospel reading. That evening, I visited Amm Sadek and found him overflowing with spiritual joy, his face radiant with delight. He greeted me eagerly and said, "Blessed be Your name, O God! I am astounded by the love of God and His unbelievable work."

I asked him what had happened to make him say such words.

He answered, as though confessing, "During your sermon today, I had very comforting thoughts that I knew would benefit the congregation present in the church, so I prayed and asked Christ to place these very thoughts in your heart, that you might utter them. And, astonishingly, you immediately used them, word for word! I started to kneel in the sanctuary, kissing the feet of the Lord, thanking Him for His grace that is working in us and for the Holy Spirit who strengthens us and answers our prayers."

In Sickness

Later in his life, Amm Sadek suffered from severe chest allergies that prevented him from going to church. From his home, he would follow the liturgy in spirit, word by word, movement by movement. Though absent in body, his soul remained fully immersed in the fellowship and worship of the church. He would take Communion at home in fear and awe of the Lord. He offered great love when he addressed Christ with tearful eyes, saying, "My Beloved, You come to this lowly house to Your poor slave." Despite his frail body and severe illness, he frequently knelt down, barely able to catch his breath. His fervent spirit never ceased offering worship, sacrifice, and love to Him who loved us until the end (Jn 13:1).

The Living Word of God

In his last days, he suffered greatly from his illness, struggling to breathe. Yet, the moment one of his spiritual children would begin speaking with him about the word of eternal life, his breathing would regulate, as if he had no illness at all.

His brother's wife, whom he always called "my sister," would often say to him in amazement, "My brother, I truly don't understand you. Just moments ago, you were on the verge of death, and now you are speaking! Why don't you be quiet for a while and rest?"

He would smile gently and reply, "My sister, do you not know that the word of God is living and life-giving? As I speak it with my lips, it brings me life."

The Final Days

In his last days, Amm Sadek was occupied with one thought that filled his life and stamped itself on all his words and meditations: the end of the world.

"Little children, it is the last hour" (1 Jn 2:18), he would say.

It was as though the Lord had revealed to him in advance that his departure was near and that he would soon cast off his earthly dwelling. He constantly urged his spiritual children to remain watchful and prepared for the coming of the Bridegroom. There is no greater example of this encouragement than this profound paragraph that starts a letter he wrote to one of his spiritual children abroad:

My beloved son,

As the Great Lent approaches, grace sets before my soul a rich table, providing me with nourishment to sustain me as I run toward my Beloved. But because of my weakness and negligence, I often miss much of this gift. Yet, in the new year, His grace grants me what I failed to enjoy in the past. I have pleaded with Christ, for the sake of my love towards Him, to seat you, His beloved, next to your old father, so that you, my son, may draw sufficient strength for running along the spiritual path to meet the blessed Christ.

Excerpts from Letters to His Spiritual Children

My beloved son in the Lord Jesus,

❖ The life of Christ, glory be to Him, is for you. It is revealed in the Holy Scriptures and in the lives of the saints. Therefore, do not study it merely as *about* Christ, but rather, study it *in yourself*, for you have put on Christ. All His attributes, emotions, and words are to be manifested in you and through you. Study His life in the lives of the saints, knowing that everything they attained is also for you, so that you may follow their example in subduing and disciplining the will, until your will merges with the will of Christ. Thus, as He was revealed in them, He will also be revealed in you.

❖ When you read the Bible, you are in the presence of Christ Himself. He is the subject of everything you read. Thus, do not approach the Bible merely as a reader, but rather as one surrendering to the work of grace within you. Therefore, read little, but meditate much, so that what you read may become life within you. Strive to live out what you read, believing that the word of God is, in itself, spirit and life. This divine power that works with your spirit will bring forth life—that is, the life of the beloved Savior in you.

❖ Do not ever read or listen to anything but the spiritual teachers, saints, and children of your Church, whom the Holy Spirit works within. But you cannot have the discernment to do this unless you yourself live a spiritual life.

❖ Let your life be a life of unceasing prayer, filled with love and thanksgiving. For your prayer is your life, and your life is your prayer. This is the meaning of your spiritual communion with Christ—that everything you read, say, do, or perceive, whether externally or internally, becomes an element of your prayer, praise, thanksgiving, and waves of love toward Christ the King, in response to His works of salvation for you and for all mankind.

❖ Train your spirit to receive the signs of the Holy Spirit that are working in you, in everything, in everybody, at every event, at every time, in every place, and under every condition. Your continuous prayer will be a link between your spirit and Christ's by the Holy Spirit, as long as you communicate with Him according to His will and not yours, making His will supreme above all. Then, you will be able to receive His spiritual dialogue, inflamed with His love for you, in response to your prayers to Him.

❖ Always resist your own desires by acting with the power of the Holy Spirit, inflamed with zeal against your own will and against every self-will that interacts with you. Wage a fierce war against the body and the world by following the commandments of Christ the King. His godly Spirit, who you live by, is at odds with the spirit of the world, crushing it, along with all the whims and desires of the body, so they will not have any part in you at all. As you receive Christ, every bodily and worldly loss will turn into gain (Phil 3:7–8). This is how we can easily transform everything and every condition into a prayer of thanksgiving, glorifying the name of the beloved Redeemer.

❖ Be cautious with your words. Speak only when your speech expresses the work of grace within you, in others, or in any given matter.

❖ Be cautious in your interactions with people. Let your connections with others be driven by your relationship with Christ, for the sake of your salvation and theirs. He is very patient, forgiving, and loving towards sinners, while also purifying and nurturing the souls of the righteous.

❖ Let prayer precede everything that comes out of your mouth, in every matter and movement. Your faith will be fulfilled as you encounter Christ in all things. Thus, everything will end in the prayer of thanksgiving and the glorification of the name of the Lord, in joy that cannot be taken away from you.

❖ Beware of human standards, for the wisdom of men is foolishness to God (1 Cor 3:19). Be cautious of being satisfied with yourself, for such satisfaction stems from your own will, which is tainted by pride and guided by the spirit of darkness. Rather, let the work of the Holy Spirit alone, aimed at pleasing Christ in you, complete whatever is lacking in you (Phil 1:6).

❖ Know, my beloved son, that the children of God are known by their spiritual lives, which are liberated from all that is bodily, earthly, or worldly. By their very nature, they see no purpose in such things, for they find them worthless, instinctively repelling them. Above all, they regard Christ alone as their entire lives, finding stability in abiding in Him, just as He abides in them (Jn 15:4–5). They contrast sharply with the children of the world, who consider worldly and earthly possessions to be all they need to sustain their lives. This is why they do not respond to the word of God and why the sons of God do not respond to all the temptations of the world and body. Those who are alive in the spirit are dead to the body, and those who are alive in the body are dead to the spirit, for faith is life, and life proclaims faith. The choice is between the worship of God or the worship of the world. These are the directives of grace to you, my beloved son. You will not benefit from them, and you cannot execute any of them, unless you strip away the power of your body and that of the spirit of the world. Then, you can substitute this power with the intent, desire, and action of the Holy Spirit. If you do this—and you can do it immediately if you choose—you will instantly ignite your heart with love for Christ, as you sense His overwhelming love for you, which all creation proclaims. At that moment, the matters of the body and of the world will lose their effect on you and their value to your soul, making it easy for you to shed their power off of you and move forward—not by your own strength, but by the power of the Holy Spirit, who fills you while you are on the path of heavenly glories with the Beloved. You will drink, get full of the richness of your Father, and receive His blessings. Glory be to Him forever. Amen.

His Death

After he completed his good race (2 Tim 4:7), spending his sojourning days in prayers, fasts, vigils, tears, love, chastity, observance of his Master's commandments, and faithfulness with the few talents entrusted to him (Mt 25:14–30), the Lord permitted him to leave the toil of this world on November 6, 1969 (Paope 27). Those present were comforted by a pleasant scent of incense emanating from his body. Thus, he departed to join the righteous in the heavenly Paradise.

His Burial

During this time, God allowed us to start building the new Church of St. Takla Haymanot in Ibrahimia, and, since it was near the house of Amm Sadek, we decided to pray his funeral there. This was the first time we had prayed over a body in that church.

We prayed the deacon's funeral prayers over him, according to his rank, but we were delayed for a while because the church was not yet prepared. We couldn't find the prayer book we needed, so Fr. Bishoy went to retrieve a copy from our church in Sporting.

After the funeral prayer, Fr. Bishoy gave a deep and spiritual sermon, suitable to the stature of Amm Sadek. His pure body was carried in a procession inside the church and then placed in a car to be taken to the cemetery.

The car I was in beat the others to the burial site. The grave was open, and Amm Sadek's body had yet to arrive. We stood waiting for a long time, but, to our surprise, no one came. Then, one of the servants informed us that they had returned Amm Sadek's body to the church. How could this be?

We learned that his relatives, who had arrived from Cairo, refused to have the casket transported and forced the driver to turn back around. They insisted on taking his body with them, as they could not accept burying him in Alexandria. They believed that his body should remain with them in Cairo, bringing blessings to everyone, as we all knew the extent of his holiness. Those present at the funeral tried to dissuade them from this decision, but it was to no avail. Since it was impossible to make it to Cairo to bury him before sunset, they laid his coffin in the church overnight. This served as a great comfort to his spiritual children, who gathered around it, praying and reading psalms and praises until the morning. So, without human intention, but rather by divine arrangement, the passing of this righteous man was celebrated in a similar fashion to that meant for the patriarchs and bishops, which is marked by vigilance, prayers, and praises.

In the morning, we prayed the Divine Liturgy and then traveled with him to Cairo, where his body was laid in its final resting place, awaiting the last trumpet, which will mark his resurrection from the dead in Christ. On that day, his perishable, mortal body will put on incorruption and immortality, as the Lord transforms our humble bodies to be like His glorified body because He can subdue everything to His will.

May the blessing of this righteous man be with us. Amen.

FEED MY SHEEP

CHAPTER TWO

Amm Abdelmalek Tawadros

This righteous man lived among us in Alexandria for many years. Previously, he had worked in Sudan. When Fr. Bishoy Kamel was ordained, he lived for some time in a small apartment in Amm Abdelmalek's family house. Fr. Bishoy got to know him closely and bore witness to his piety and righteousness.

Amm Abdelmalek was a man of noble character married to a virtuous woman. He and his wife, who were childless, lived a holy life filled with the fear of God. His two unmarried sisters also lived with them, and this house was an example of the Christian life in its love and humility. It was the embodiment of this verse: "Behold, how good and how pleasant it is For brethren to dwell together in unity!" (Ps 133:1).

Amm Abdelmalek was the secret blessing of the house because he was very close to God. He was exceptionally organized in his life, and his spirituality reflected this same meticulous order. He regularly prayed the Agpeya prayers and memorized all the psalms included in them.[3] He was consistent with his Bible readings every morning and every night. He read the entire Bible twice a year and memorized many chapters. His mind was always occupied with the Gospel, both when he was alone and when he was in the company of others or having conversations. The Gospel filled his whole life.

Everybody wondered how a busy man like him, who was responsible for the management of his house, could find time for such spirituality. This is the question that is often asked by those who find excuses, but for those who have tasted the sweetness of God's word, time is plentiful and blessed, and the Gospel takes precedence over all other necessities.

The Church of St. Mark

Daily liturgies were held in the Church of St. Mark, and Amm Abdelmalek was known for his renowned discipline in attending them. In the early 1950s, he committed to regularly attending the liturgy, which ended around 8:00 a.m. every day. He prepared himself with steadfastness and strength in all aspects of his life to keep this commitment; despite the

---

[3] The *Agpeya* is the daily prayer book of the Coptic Orthodox Church, containing a series of prayers, psalms, and Gospel readings for the seven canonical hours. These prayers commemorate events in the life of Christ and serve as a guide for spiritual discipline and worship throughout the day.

distance between his home and the church, Amm Abdelmalek was always among the first to rise early for the Lord.

The Vicar

It is customary for the pope, who serves as the bishop of the great city of Alexandria, to appoint a representative to oversee the affairs of Alexandria in his absence. Usually, this representative, called the vicar, is chosen from among the monks.

As Amm Abdelmalek went to the Church of St. Mark every day, he decided to start presenting a daily gift to the acting vicar, who resided there. Amm Abdelmalek went to church early every morning with a container of prepared food, and he would quietly place it in front of the vicar's cell. In the silence and darkness of the early morning, nobody saw him. He asked one of the attendants in the Patriarchate to return the empty container to him and not to tell anyone about this secret deed.[4] The attendant obeyed him, and many of the vicars received Amm Abdelmalek's gift without knowing his name or identity.

In 1954, a new monk was appointed as the vicar for Pope Yousab II, and, when he found the food container every morning upon opening his cell door, he was greatly surprised

---

[4] There are two Patriarchates in Egypt—one in Alexandria and one in Cairo. The Cairo Patriarchate is referred to in a later chapter ("Deacon Youssef Habib").

and wanted to find the person behind the act.[5] He asked everyone who worked in the Patriarchate. When he asked the attendant in charge of giving the container back to Amm Abdelmalek, the attendant only replied, "One of the faithful people," which is what Amm Abdelmalek had told him to say.

Determined to uncover the mystery, the monk woke up very early one day—around 3 in the morning—opened his cell door slightly, and stood behind it, waiting for this righteous man. His heart was moved by this hidden act of love, and he longed to meet its doer. Right on time, Amm Abdelmalek arrived, carrying his basket, and quietly placed it at the cell door, unaware that he was being watched. As he put the basket down, the monk bent down to kiss him.

The vicar later told him, "Please do not exert yourself," to which Amm Abdelmalek replied, "Please do not deprive me of this blessing."

When Pope Yousab II departed in 1956, he was succeeded by Pope Kyrillos VI, who loved Alexandria and spent a great deal of time there. Amm Abdelmalek continued to attend the daily liturgies, as was his custom. The pope was friendly with him and was always happy to see him. He felt Amm Abdelmalek's great piety, devoutness, and spirituality and

---

[5] This monk was Fr. Matthew the Poor. He served as the vicar from March 1954 to May 1955, after which he willingly left to go back to the Monastery of St. Mary El-Sourian.

delighted in his presence. He often invited Amm Abdelmalek to his patriarchal cell to have coffee with him.

Amm Abdelmalek continued to provide food for the vicar, as well as for the monks staying with the pope in Alexandria's Papal Secretariat, in complete secrecy.

With Those of Differing Opinions

Amm Abdelmalek frequently spoke with God and about Him, but he rarely spoke with people or about people. He was often in the company of Pope Kyrillos VI; he was close to the pope's heart and beloved by all the fathers at the papal residence.

During this time, disagreements often occurred among the bishops and monks; there were many differing opinions. People talked a great deal about these differences, which often led to bickering and disputes. Meetings in church circles were characterized by much talk and, sometimes, by insubordination.

As the people divided themselves, taking one side or the other, Amm Abdelmalek never participated in these matters, remaining a friend to all. He was loved by everybody and never got swept up by any particular current. His heart was vast enough to embrace everyone.

Amm Abdelmalek never spoke to Pope Kyrillos VI about the issues. He was a friend to those who disagreed with the pope, and the pope knew this. In fact, if the pope ever voiced complaints about certain people in Amm Abdelmalek's presence, this righteous man would respond with a humble smile, "You are their father and they are all your children. They all seek the good of the church."

He was a man of peace who maintained a pure heart untainted by hatred or politics. With his simple and wise heart, he remained free and impartial, making himself a servant to all. Thus, Amm Abdelmalek became a source of blessing to many, even those whose opinions differed from his. He did not express bias, nor did he flatter his superiors. Instead, pure Christian love, free of ulterior motives, filled his heart.

Everyone genuinely loved and trusted him. Through his behavior, he led many to peace. Truly, the life of this righteous man can serve as a lesson for many.

The Work of the Devil

One evening, Amm Abdelmalek was visiting his friend's house in Sudan. His friend was hosting some acquaintances, among whom was a man of many tricks. The devil had enlisted this man for his purposes, and he amazed the attendees with extraordinary acts.

One of his feats was to bring any item from a person's home. He declared, "I am now ready to bring each of you something from your house."

One by one, those present asked him for objects, and indeed, he brought each person whatever they requested from their home.

As this was happening, Amm Abdelmalek remained calm and composed, while the others laughed and cheered loudly.

When it was Amm Abdelmalek's turn, the man asked him, "What would you like from your home? I can bring it to you in a moment and place it on this table, just like I did for the others."

Amm Abdelmalek responded with great politeness and humility, "Thank you, but I do not want anything."

The man, encouraged by the devil and seemingly intent on embarrassing Amm Abdelmalek, insisted, "You must ask for something."

Amm Abdelmalek replied calmly, "There is no need for embarrassment."

But the man grew more persistent. As his demands escalated, Amm Abdelmalek finally said, with profound calmness, "If you can, bring me the small book that I keep under the pillow in my room."

This book was his Agpeya, the book of prayers. The man took longer than usual in his attempt to retrieve it. The people present watched, wondering why he was delayed. Time passed, and their eyes remained fixed, waiting—why had he failed this time?

The man then said, "I cannot bring you this book! But you must ask for something else."

Everyone was greatly astonished and afraid, wondering what it was that the devil could not approach. They asked Amm Abdelmalek, who answered them simply and with great humility, "That is the room where I pray, and this is my prayer book. Demons fear prayer and flee from the sign of the cross."

A True Story about the Sacraments

Amm Abdelmalek told me that he knew a saintly priest in the countryside who was filled with the fruits of the Spirit. During the Holy Liturgy, someone came and informed the priest that one of the elders of the church was going to Jerusalem.

The priest asked the old man in question, "Why do you want to do this, my son?"

The elder replied, "I want to see the light of Christ."

The priest then asked a deacon to bring him an unlit candle. He lifted the veil on the chalice, brought the candle close to it, and it miraculously lit. Handing the candle back to the deacon, the priest said, "This is the light of Christ, who is with us every day on the altar."

Amm Abdelmalek treasured in his memory stories of many righteous people like this priest. He lived among them, loved them, and followed their path of holiness, straying far from frivolity and worldly talk. As long as he lived, he never sat in the seat of mockers (Ps 1:1) or spoke ill of anyone. His life was adorned with many virtues, as testified by all who knew him. He finally slept in the Lord after completing his good fight (2 Tim 4:7). He quietly departed to the Father's bosom in peace and serenity.

CHAPTER THREE

A Model of True Repentance

He was completely ordinary in every aspect. Nothing— neither his occupation nor his lifestyle— distinguished him from the other men of his generation. He was a schoolteacher, and he moved from one city to another by virtue of his profession. After he married and had children, he settled down in a city that was situated along the Nile in Upper Egypt. The main form of recreation in this small city was a cinema, but the man did not go there very often; he preferred to go on boat rides on the Nile with his children and a few friends. He was not very religious and did not go to church regularly. He frequently erred and fell, but he was very kind in heart and extremely sensitive.

He confessed later that he had not known the meaning of repentance until this incident. One day, during a school break, this man, along with a large group, was happily cruising the Nile on a small boat. The young people, playfully having fun, all moved to one side of the boat, causing it to become unbalanced and turn over, thus throwing everybody on board into the deepest part of the Nile.

The man could not swim, so he cried out to God from the depths of his heart. His only son was with him, while his wife and daughters were at home, having decided not to go out that day. The man embraced his son, convinced that this would be the end. There was no time to think, and he was overcome by a great sense of weakness.

He later said, "I felt that I had never cried to God from the depth of my heart as I did in that moment."

Immediately, he felt two compassionate hands lifting him, with his only son in his arms, and bringing him to shore. That man and his son were the only two people to survive that day.

For this man, this was the beginning of a life of sanctity. He prayed like he had never prayed before, avoiding and despising all earthly vanities. The world lost all value in his eyes, and a higher infinite scope opened up before him. He found himself, at last, and the Lord gave him a new life filled with new days. Since he was a sincere man with a simple heart, he used these new days to store up treasures for himself in heaven (Mt 6:20).

Every afternoon when he returned home from work, he would enter his room to pray the ninth hour psalms from the Agpeya. Then, he would have his first meal of the day (as an offering of thanksgiving, he had vowed a fast of repentance to God). Afterward, he would rest for a short time before entering his study, which he had now dedicated to prayer. There, he would remain, gazing toward heaven, praying deeply from his heart, enjoying the psalms and praises, immersing himself in the Holy Bible, and learning at the feet of the saints. The man persevered in this heavenly life, enjoying every part of it, like a thirsty man drinking deeply from the Spring of Life; his spiritual fervor increased every day.

One night, as he was praying and gazing up to heaven, it was as though the ceiling vanished completely, and the heavens opened up before him.

The man was overwhelmed by the abundance of God's love. He was overcome by feelings of humility and unworthiness. The Lord had allowed him to see the unseen.

The man kept all these matters in his heart and did not share them with anyone on the face of the earth.

The Liturgies

After the boat incident, the man began going to church regularly. He attended the liturgies, evening prayers, and spiritual meetings, all while in a tranquil, gentle state of mind.

Many attributed this behavior to the immediate effect of the accident, assuming that this lifestyle would last for some time before he would go back to his natural state and old life, like anyone else who is affected in the short-term by a traumatic event or "like a man observing his natural face in a mirror; for he observes himself, goes away, and immediately forgets what kind of man he was" (Jas 1:23–24). But the transformation of this man's heart was not of the temporary kind. He had come to understand the reality of the world's impermanence and experience the joy of a constant life with God, not through listening to sermons and talks, but through living it.

The Divine Liturgy, which had once been boring and tedious to him, became the sweetest and most desirable experience for him on earth. In the past, it had been dull and burdensome, and he could hardly endure staying in church. Now, the church was paradise, and the liturgy was his way of partaking of the Tree of Life.

Over the years, all who knew him testified that he had become an example of the Christian way of life and the embodiment of the commandments of the Gospel. He was pleasant to everyone, meek without pretense, and tender-hearted toward all. His daily life was filled with the spirit of prayer, humility, and selfless service.

He received comfort from divine sights and spiritual visions given to him through God's grace. One day, as was his custom, the man entered the church to pray the Divine Liturgy. He lifted his eyes in prayer as the priest was praying the Commemoration of the Saints, and he saw each saint enter the sanctuary one by one. Every time the priest mentioned a name, that saint appeared, joining the heavenly choir.

The man's tears flowed freely as he stood beside the altar. The words uttered in every liturgy, "Whenever we stand in Your holy sanctuary, we are considered standing in heaven," became a reality.[6] Truly, "How awesome is this place! This is none other than the house of God, and this is the gate of heaven!" (Gen 28:17).

These manifestations led to the man's increased humility and awareness of his sins and unworthiness. He grew in virtue and took comfort in prayer.

The Wiles of the Devil

"Be sober, be vigilant; because your adversary the devil walks about like a roaring lion, seeking whom he may devour. Resist him, steadfast in the faith" (1 Pet 5:8–9).

The enemy ground his teeth in rage whenever he saw the man increasing in virtue. The man was not experienced in spiritual warfare, and he was not a disciple of a wise elder in a monastery, nor was he under the guidance of a discerning mentor in the church. Instead, he was a simple man supported by grace, running the spiritual race with all his energy and love. The accuser of humanity has been known to test the saints and was granted authority as the prince of this world (Jn 14:30). If

---

[6] These words are found in certain litanies of the Agpeya, including one in the third hour prayer, which is recited during the Divine Liturgy of St. Basil.

he had fought against the great patriarchs, who was this simple man to stand against him?

So, the devil started spreading his nets and wicked wiles around the man. He began by giving him bodily complaints—symptoms of illness, weakness, and the excessive need for rest and food. These were small steps towards laziness, and then, lukewarm prayers. Gradually, the world crept into his life—just as water slowly seeps into a large ship through a tiny hole. As time passed, the devil succeeded in his schemes, and the man returned to his former ways.

From time to time, he would awaken and recall the glory of his days of repentance and life with God. He would gather what little strength he had left to stand and pray. But his prayers were weak and lukewarm. It was as though he prayed merely out of obligation, without any flavor or joy. The liturgy and the Bible had no effect on him. He would lament, regret, and yearn for the days of old, but, day by day, everything slipped away—even his remorse and emotional stirring. It was as if his conscience had died.

And so, he fell into his old sins and returned to his companions in evil.

Is There a Way Back?

God, in His bountiful mercy and His benevolence toward His beloved, does not abandon the righteous in their weakness or distress, nor does He allow the devil to triumph over His children in the end. Instead, He leads His children along the path of triumph through Christ the Lord and restores to them the years the locusts have eaten (Joel 2:25).

Divine grace once again visited this man in his misery, and he returned to the spring of tears and to secret prayer. As he prayed to God in his later years, now approaching his 60s, he would cry out with a broken spirit, "Do I have a place of acceptance?"

And so, life began to flow once more through his soul, reviving the man from his spiritual death. He resumed his journey along the path to eternal life. Like our father Isaac, he began to re-dig the old wells the enemy had filled, uncovering the Wells of the Spirit one by one, until he reached the Well of Seven, the well of satisfaction (Gen 26:17–33).

As a respectable old man, he came to me for confession. As he spoke, abundant tears flowed in a way I had never seen before.

He said, "Now I know that the Lord is good, kind, and accepting of sinners. I have realized that no matter how great our sins are, the blood of our Lord Jesus Christ cleanses us from all sin. Where sin abounds, grace abounds much more [Rom 5:20]. I thought there was no way back to the days of my early repentance, but what I did not deserve after the abundance of my sins, grace has restored to me."

I asked him what made him say this, and he replied, "My visions of the divine and heavenly revelations had ceased for a long time due to the magnitude of my sins and my spiritual lukewarmness. I thought there was no return to my former spiritual state. But I entered the church yesterday, and, to my great astonishment, my spiritual sight was opened again. I saw the sanctuary filled with the spirits of the saints and angels. The sight was beyond description. My soul returned to its earlier humility, joy, and contrition. I became certain that God balances the weight of our sins with the abundance of His love, and that the door of repentance remains open even to the worst of sinners."

A Happy Ending

The Lord adorned this man's life with suffering in his final days. He gained favor before the Lord every day for his great patience, thanksgiving, and constant praises, until he finally joined the ranks of shining heavenly hosts and began to enjoy the fullness of what he had tasted during his life on earth.

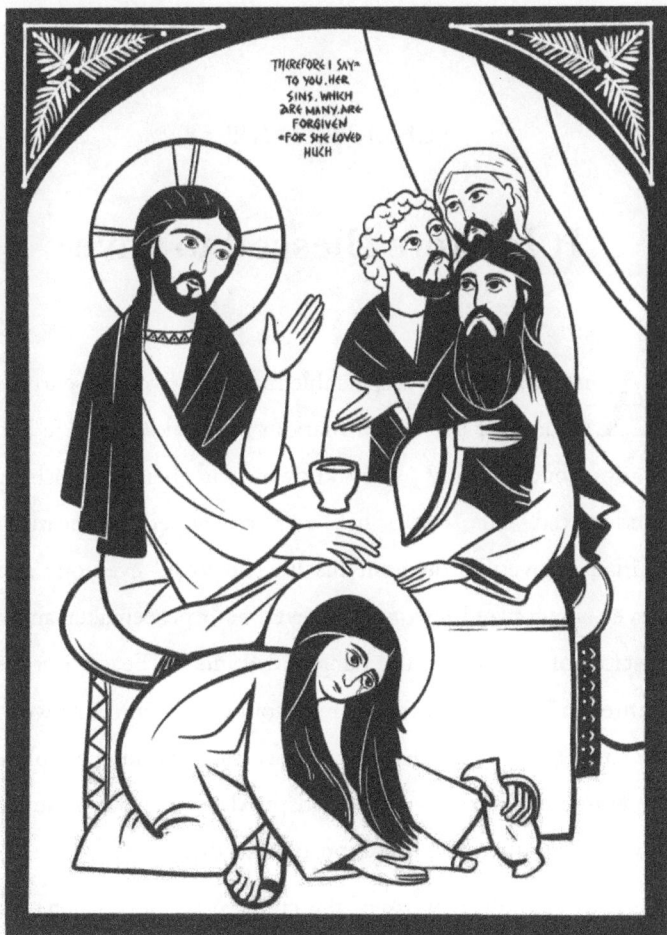

CHAPTER FOUR

It Is More Blessed to Give

A mm Farid was a respectable man who lived close to the Church of the Virgin Mary in Zeitoun, Cairo. He had many children and was known for being unusually kindhearted. His entire life was enveloped in heartfelt Christian love. Throughout his life, he loved everyone and never antagonized anyone, but lived as a peacemaker and a disciple of his Master, the King and Prince of Peace. For his entire family, he was a balm for all wounds. Wherever he went, he spread peace and love. It was even said that in every place he entered, his presence alone inspired those around him to love one another deeply and pure-heartedly.

This is the true work of the children of God: when they live according to the commandments and enjoy the blessings of grace, they share these blessings simply and abundantly with others through their actions and lives, more than through their words. This is how Amm Farid lived; his words were few, but his presence was effective.

Amm Farid planted such fruit in his children. They loved one another wholeheartedly, and no earthly issue tarnished their relationships with each other. They remained close, despite the physical distance between them. Their beautiful, strong bonds of true love were credited to their father, who lived faithfully, adhering to Christ's commandments all the days of his sojourn on earth.

Another beautiful holy sign adorned the days of his life on earth: the man was fully committed to the Lord's words, "It is more blessed to give than to receive" (Acts 20:35), and grace constantly provided him with opportunities to give, which he seized with joy. In this way, he grew in virtue and generosity to all.

His giving went beyond the traditional concept. He was remarkably gentle and extraordinarily compassionate. Many times, his children witnessed him calling out to a poor-looking street vendor near the Virgin Mary Church. He would ask what the man was selling and the price. If the vendor said, for example, "20 piasters for an ounce," or "20 piasters for a kilo," Amm Farid would reply, "No, my son, that's too little. It should be 25 piasters. Weigh four kilos for me."

When Amm Farid overheard someone objecting, as usual, to the high price or the poor quality of the goods, he would quietly signal to the vendor, saying, "Don't worry about what they're saying. Accept what they offer, and I will make it up to you." After the buyer would leave, Amm Farid would quickly go to the window, toss the money to the vendor, and say, "Go, my son, and may God bless you." Amm Farid believed that the Lord was pleased with sacrifices of this kind.

Amm Farid's life was marked by wonderful humility. He always chose the lowest seat, according to the Lord's commandments (Lk 14:10). He served everyone, always putting himself last, preferring others over himself, and making sacrifices for the happiness of others—a rare sight in our times.

Prayers, liturgies, and holy fasts were the pillars of his life. The psalms, which he meditated on day and night, were his delight, and he was always exceedingly blessed with heavenly grace and support.

A Radiant End

As the days of this righteous man's earthly sojourn drew to a close, he fell slightly ill. The Lord revealed to him the day of his departure from this world, just as He had done for the great saints, three days in advance. The man called his wife and all his children to gather around him. Holding his wife's hand, he kissed it and said to her, "Forgive me, for you are more righteous than I am."

He then began reminding his children of the great promise that love never fails and advising them to cling to Christ until the very last breath. They were all amazed at his strange behavior. They wept and said, "You are in good health, and all will be well."

He replied, "Tomorrow, I will partake of the Holy Mysteries, and the day after, Christ will come to visit me."

And so it was. On the following day, a priest came and gave him Holy Communion. On the day after that, this righteous man departed to the heavenly dwellings, his good deeds following him. He departed in prayer, saying, "Holy God, Holy…"

Those who knew him testified that they had never heard him utter a single idle or vain word. Thus, he was found worthy to repeat the praises of the seraphim (Is 6:3) with his last breath, singing this song with the host of those redeemed before the throne of Christ. The word "holy" was the last word spoken by the tongue of this man, who lived in holiness until his departure.

Before his departure, he told his daughter, who came from Alexandria to be by his bedside, "Tell Fr. Tadros and Fr. Salib to pray for me, that the Lord may grant my soul rest in the Paradise of Joy."

Remarkably, at the time of his passing, Frs. Tadros and Salib traveled to attend his funeral without having been informed about it beforehand. It was Christ who fulfilled this righteous man's final request, bearing witness that he had found favor before God and that every word he spoke came to pass.

CHAPTER FIVE

She Went up to Heaven

L aila was a woman in the prime of her youth with no apparent qualities that set her apart from others. She was completely ordinary in every aspect. She wasn't a Sunday School teacher, nor did she have a prominent role or a well-known name. She was simply an ordinary young woman who went to church in Cairo.

After she married a relative from Alexandria, she lived near our church in Sporting. She attended the liturgies and evening prayers but did not socialize much. From time to time, she came to confess to God before me during the Vespers prayer. I often admired this sister for her pure heart and transparent soul. Despite becoming the mother of two children, she retained her innocent heart and soul, which were untainted by the world.

In her married life, she was a noble example of faithfulness and love. She practiced God's commandment, "do not let the sun go down on your wrath" (Eph 4:26). She adhered to it literally, never letting a day pass without resolving any argument she may have had with her husband. Whenever there was a misunderstanding, she hastened to forgive and apologize. Thus, her heart remained pure. Didn't the Lord say, "Blessed are the pure in heart" (Mt 5:8)?

Her Son's Attachment to Her

Laila's daughter was 4 years old, and her son was 2 years old. This young boy was unusually attached to her. Their bond was a topic of discussion among those around her. The boy couldn't bear to be apart from her for even a moment—not even when she went to the bathroom. The family expressed concern about the situation, but she remained calm, always filled with peace, never disturbed by anything.

An Unexpected Departure

One day, her husband returned home from work in the afternoon, as usual, to find everything in the house clean and organized. She had prepared the meal and set the table; everything was perfect.

They ate together before her husband rested for a while. He then got ready to leave for his evening shift, but she said to him, "Don't go out today."

Surprised, he asked, "Why?"

She replied, "I need you."

"What do you need? Don't you know I have work obligations and can't be late?"

She insisted. He pressed her for an explanation, until she finally said, "I'm going to die today."

He stood there, stunned and unable to process what he had just heard.

"What are you talking about?" he exclaimed. "You are in perfect health and at the prime of your life. Your energy is evident in all the work you've done today."

She calmly said, "Please, this is what will happen."

She had barely spoken these words when she sat on a nearby chair, and her complexion turned pale. Within moments, she lost consciousness.

Her husband stood in utter disbelief, unable to comprehend what was happening. He began to scream while their children cried in distress at the tragic scene. Desperately, he slapped her cheeks, hoping she would wake up. After a few moments, she opened her eyes, vomited, took a breath, and returned to consciousness.

Her husband was overwhelmed with joy and exclaimed, "Thank God you're okay! I was losing my mind just moments ago!"

She interrupted him, saying, "Listen, I truly died and went to Paradise. I met many of those who have departed, and I spoke with *Baba* [her father, who had passed away years earlier]. He told me, 'No, my daughter, you are still young, and your children are little. Go back.' But no…I know that I will die soon. Heaven is beautiful. Please, hold on to God, keep His commandments, and raise the children in the fear of the Lord."

With those words, she rested in the Lord. Her husband tried everything humanly possible to revive her, but the matter had already been decided by the Lord.

The Lord Protects the Little Children

A few hours later, the house was full of people. One pressing matter loomed: the problem of the little child and his great attachment to his mother. Most of those present believed that the boy would not survive without her. They thought he would die from grief, as he could not bear even a moment apart from her—how could he endure her absence forever?

But God, in His divine work to honor this righteous mother and to comfort all those around her, demonstrated that, even in heaven, she could care for her children by interceding for them. The Lord granted the little boy an extraordinary calmness. He did not cry for his mother or even ask about her.

This was reminiscent of the story of a martyred catechumen. When she was imprisoned in preparation for her martyrdom, the guards detained her infant child and refused to feed him for an entire day. They brought the crying child to her in an attempt to influence her maternal emotions and weaken her resolve, but, through her fervent prayers and by God's grace, the infant stopped crying, as if comforted by a divine presence. A similar divine miracle occurred in the life of this family. Months after the mother's passing, when photographs were shown to the little boy, he could identify all the other relatives and call them by name, but when he saw a picture of his mother, it was as though he didn't recognize her. He would simply remain silent.

The boy lived a normal life, and the Lord poured extraordinary peace into his heart and into the hearts of Laila's family. The story of this righteous mother's departure became a cause of repentance and a source of comfort for many.

CHAPTER SIX

Only Five Days Remain

A mm Michel was an elderly, unmarried layman who had retired from his position in a government office. He dedicated his life to others, serving them sacrificially and selflessly. For many years, he consistently attended the liturgies at St. Mark Church *(El-Morkoseya)*. Only extreme circumstances could prevent him from going.

Fr. Matta would visit Amm Michel in his home, which he shared with some relatives. This priest enjoyed the company of Amm Michel. They spoke of the wonderful works of God and meditated on the living and life-giving word.

In the last year of Amm Michel's life, illness confined him to his bed. Although he loved the Divine Liturgy deeply and his heart's desire was to attend it every day, he accepted his illness with great humility and thanksgiving.

Fr. Matta comforted him with words of grace and with the Eucharist, which he brought to Amm Michel every Monday. After giving him the Eucharist with the utmost reverence and worship, Fr. Matta would sit with him to share comforting, edifying conversation over a light breakfast.

During his last months, Amm Michel requested to receive the Eucharist twice a week. He apologized to Fr. Matta for the inconvenience this could have caused him. But Fr. Matta's love never grew weary; he went to Amm Michel with joy, carrying the body and blood of our Lord, who is the Bread of Eternal Life.

As Amm Michel was receiving the Eucharist one day, he gave thanks for Christ's bountiful grace and His kind and wonderful descent to man. With a spiritual glow in his eyes, he said to Fr. Matta, "You have truly worked hard for me. May Christ grant you the heavenly reward on my behalf. Please, do not trouble yourself with me any longer—I feel that the ship is nearing the shore, and my sojourn is almost over. Only five days remain."

Fr. Matta and the deacon who had accompanied him that day listened in astonishment and disbelief.

Fr. Matta asked Amm Michel, "How can you say this?"

Amm Michel replied, "Monday, Tuesday, Wednesday, and Thursday will pass, and on Friday, I will leave the prison of the body."

Fr. Matta sat down as usual and blessed the food, and they ate thankfully. They spoke of the kingdom of God, the promises of Christ, and the eternal joy reserved for the holy.

Fr. Matta and the deacon took their leave from his home in Christian love.

On his way out, Fr. Matta said, "I will come the day after tomorrow."

The man humbly replied, "Do not trouble yourself or waste your time."

On Friday, at the time previously appointed and revealed by God, this just man's soul was released like Simeon the Elder's (Lk 2:29). When Fr. Matta went to visit him that day, he found that the man had reposed a few hours earlier. Fr. Matta realized that it was not strange that God should have faithful witnesses who lived in the world but were not of the world.

CHAPTER SEVEN

Your Prayer Was Heard

About 14 years ago, I went out to visit some members of the congregation. I looked at my small pocket agenda, where I kept a record of the addresses of the people I visited. At the time, street names were very similar in pronunciation and spelling; for example, there were Hermopolis vs. Memphis, Tanis vs. Menes, and other pairs like these. I read one of the addresses from my agenda and memorized the street name, the building number, and the apartment number.

I went to the street, found the building number I was looking for, and climbed the stairs to the third floor. I quickly realized that it was a home I had never visited before. I thought that I could be at the wrong address, so I consulted my pocket agenda and found that I was indeed on the wrong street. But I had already rung the doorbell, and I was too embarrassed to leave before the door opened.

A moment later, the door was opened, and I stood before a man in his 40s with ruffled hair.

A moment later, the door was opened, and I stood before a man in his 40s with ruffled hair.

He said, "Yes?"

I saw a Christian icon on a calendar hanging on the wall behind him, so I thought to myself, *Good. Even if I came to the wrong address, there is no harm in visiting here, for this is a Christian household.*

I asked the man, "Are you Christians?"

"Yes, we are, but how did you get our address? Who gave it to you?"

"As long as you are Christians, I can visit you."

I didn't know why, but he looked troubled. He said, "Do come in."

There was something strange in the atmosphere that I could not understand. I had never faced a situation like this before.

As soon as I entered, the man closed the door behind me and said again, with a puzzled look, "Please tell me who gave you my address."

I was very surprised and said, "May I sit down?"

"Please do."

He remained standing before me, and I calmly told him, "Please take a seat, and I will tell you."

The man sat by my side, still astonished. There was silence for a few seconds, and then I asked him, "Why are you so troubled? Have you never seen a priest before? I will not tell you how I came to you unless you first tell me why you feel the way you feel."

The man was overcome with emotion and said, "This is very strange. I can hardly believe what I am seeing. As you can see, I live alone in this apartment. I moved to Alexandria more than 20 years ago. I come from a Christian family. Before I came here, I lived in a small village, and, at that time, I was a very religious young man, living in a loving relationship with Christ. I regularly partook of the sacraments. When I finished my studies and moved to Alexandria, my spiritual life began to decline and get cold. I began to miss prayers. Then came undesirable friendships, carelessness, and a life of sin of every sort. I felt completely lost, but my conscience awakened sometimes, and I missed my life with God and my church. But I did not give these thoughts time or place, and they fizzled out instantly. More than 20 years have passed, and I have forgotten everything. Can you imagine that I have not received the Holy Communion all this time? The strange thing is that two weeks ago, all of a sudden, my feelings erupted like a volcano. I felt contrition and wanted to return to God. I truly wept, and I went back to standing in prayer. I looked for my Bible until I found it in a pile of old, neglected books. I read it with great zeal. Its words were like sharp arrows to my heart. The whole world suddenly did not matter to me. I wanted nothing from it."

I interrupted the man, greatly perplexed, and asked, "Have you attended any church meetings lately? Have you listened to any sermons, or have you met with any servants?"

"No! Not at all! This is truly strange. My daily routine has totally changed. I come back from work every day, close the door to my apartment, and stick to my prayers, my tears, and my Bible until late in the evening. Then, I sleep, wake up in the morning, and do it all over again."

"And your friends?" I asked.

"They are truly surprised and perplexed. Every day, they try to take me back to where I was before. Some believe I am suffering from depression. Some are amazed at the changes that have occurred in my habits, my words, and my life. Anyway, I no longer care for friends or people in general. Currently, my pleasure is in the works of repentance in my bedroom. What is stranger still is that I feared my feelings may be temporary, transient, and not of God. Only yesterday, as I was praying and weeping before God, I begged Him with tears, saying, 'Lord, give me a sign that I may know You have accepted me, in spite of all my sins and transgressions.' I was so bold that I said, 'This is the sign: that You send a priest to me, that I may confess my sins before him and feel that my repentance and plea have found favor before You.'"

I was moved by these words and glorified my Lord Jesus Christ, who works in hearts through the Holy Spirit, moving His children to repent. The Lord works, even in the absence of servants, to bring back His lost sheep and find His lost coin (Lk 15:4–10).

I said to the man, whose eyes were filled with tears, "So the Lord has given you your heart's desire."

He replied, "Yes, Father, but please tell me how you came here."

I took out my little pocket agenda and pointed to the address that was written, so that he could see that the numbers of the building and apartment were the same as his, but the street was different. I said, "The Lord truly does great things for us. I made a mistake in reading the address, so I came to you as part of the Lord's plan."

We prayed together and thanked our loving Christ, the Good Shepherd and Lover of Mankind, bowing our hearts to Him who accepts sinners.

This brother then offered a confession that was recorded in heaven as a seal of true repentance accepted before God. I read him the absolution and left, glorifying God.

We met on repeated occasions after that. He attended church with a deep hunger and thirst for righteousness, and grace satisfied him according to the Lord's promise, "Blessed are those who hunger and thirst for righteousness, For they shall be filled" (Mt 5:6).

Grace restored to him the years that the locusts had eaten (Joel 2:25). He completed his days content before God and strengthened by the Holy Spirit.

✠

CHAPTER EIGHT

An Angelic Life of Service

The tram stopped near his beloved church, which had also served as his home. He had left the church an hour earlier, having received the Holy Mysteries, as was his daily custom. A crowd gathered around the tram, wondering what had happened.

The man had bowed his head and given up his spirit in a strangely peaceful manner, seated in his place on the tram. People around him thought he had fallen asleep, but when they tried to wake him up, they found that he had departed.

Thus, in angelic calmness and peace, Amm Farid left our world.[7] Those who had been with him at liturgy that day were amazed, as, just a short while earlier, he had been full of energy, showing no signs of anything unusual. But didn't the Bible say, "For what is your life? It is even a vapor that appears for a little time and then vanishes away" (Jas 4:14).

---

[7] This Amm Farid is distinct from the Amm Farid of Zeitoun, whose story is found earlier in this book.

Amm Farid's friends and relatives gathered at his house. Many memories of him began to surface in their minds. He had been a beautiful icon of Christian gentleness and meekness, following the example set by our Lord Jesus Christ. No one ever heard him raising his voice or shouting in the streets. A beautiful smile that reflected inner peace never left his face, even in the most difficult of situations.

His family recalled an extraordinary incident that occurred when Amm Farid's sister passed away. He was entitled to a considerable inheritance, and, though his material life was simple, and he needed some of that money, the man insisted— despite opposition from everyone around him—not to claim any earthly possessions. Out of his own free will, he relinquished everything to others.

The memory of his life radiated with spirituality. He was kind to all; his secret was his inner life with Christ, which was deeper than anybody knew. He had led an exalted spiritual life and maintained a loving relationship with Christ since his early youth. He woke up very early every day, at 4 a.m., and practiced his hidden spiritual activities—prayers, hymns, psalms, readings, and chants—until 7 a.m., with great joy and delight. This was his spiritual foundation for each day and his preparation to face the battles of the devil. It gave him the strength to fulfill the commandments. Nothing could deter him or change his resolve. Over the years, the roots of vigilance and prayer grew deeper in his inner life, and his outward life before people showed the fruit of his deep fellowship with God. His family testified that nothing interrupted his early rising except illness and that he had maintained this discipline for over 40 years. Thus, the spiritual source in him was always renewed, and prayer became his first instinct—as necessary to him as his own breath.

When people began to realize his secret spiritual depth, they were convinced that the spiritual life and the kingdom of God are indeed like treasures hidden in a field or pearls of great price, which, when a man found them, went and sold all he had to buy them (Mt 13:44–46).

How great is our need for the life of prayer! Prayer is how we can offer our lives as the true aroma of Christ, the treasure of the world, and the salt of the earth.

CHAPTER NINE

Poor, yet Making Many Rich

Her husband, a poor workman, passed away, leaving her with two children. She and her children lived in a small room in a poor neighborhood. This widow had no support, no money, and no male relatives. She refused to rely on anyone except Christ; she held Him to His promise that He is a husband to the widows and a father to the orphans (Ps 68:5).

Her faith in God's protection, care, and presence in her life deeply humbled me. I often wished to present the image of this poor widow to those who complain and grumble, who are neither grateful nor content, despite their abundance.

She would only accept help with great difficulty and after much insistence on my part. Eventually, she proposed that, as long as she had the strength, she should work with her own hands. In truth, her circumstances and weakness made it nearly impossible for her to work, but I encouraged her to work as a way to justify helping her, so she wouldn't feel she was receiving without giving in return. She began to do small household chores to the best of her ability, and we would try to provide her with some assistance. She would only ever accept the bare minimum she needed to survive.

The conduct of this poor widow reproached me, as I witnessed her contentment, her spiritual joy, her constant prayers and hymns as she worked with her hands, and her deep gratitude to God for even the smallest share of this life's provisions. Truly, Christ Himself filled her life with joy and blessings.

Her Sacrifices

Something strange I discovered by chance was that she saved a portion of the few coins she received for others. I once found her at the Monastery of St. Mina on a day when there were no trips to the monastery or any available transportation.

I asked, "How did you get here?"

She replied, "By train, and then I walked the rest of the way."

I learned that she had baked bread with the money she had saved and had carried it on her head all the way to the monastery.

I knew she was devoted to St. Mina, but to this extent? She spent the rest of the day in service, cleaning the monastery and mopping its floors with extraordinary joy and happiness.

She truly gave, as the Lord said, "all that she had, her whole livelihood" (Mk 12:44).

As in the Days of Elisha

One day, her youngest son, who was 6 years old, came home from school and asked for something to eat. The mother replied, "We have nothing, but take this piaster and buy some beans." That was all she had that day.

The boy went and returned with a plate of beans. He added a little salt and then asked for oil, but she had none—not even a drop. She had cleaned four bottles and turned them upside down under a small table in the room, concealed behind a curtain made from an old piece of cloth.

She apologized to her son for the lack of oil and reassured him that God would soon provide.

The boy protested, as children often do, and insisted that there *must* be oil. Gently and with a broken heart, she comforted him and encouraged him to give thanks to God.

She made the sign of the cross over the plate of beans and said, "Eat, my son."

But the boy, in his persistence, said to her, "You're hiding the oil from me, and I'm going to find it."

The boy reached behind the curtain and under the table where the bottles were. He pulled out a bottle completely full of oil.

He cried out, insisting she had hidden the oil from him. But the woman, with her spiritual discernment, quickly realized that the Lord had performed a miracle for her. She answered her son wisely, "Forgive me, my son, I forgot it." She then placed the oil before him and said, "We must give thanks to God." They prayed, and he ate.

Later that day, she came to me rejoicing and praising God. She had found all four bottles full of oil. She sent two bottles to the Monastery of St. Mina, gave one to St. George Church, and kept one for herself. She kept this miracle in her heart and told no one else about it because she felt that God's care for her and His works in her life were very personal and not to be shared widely. The woman believed that God had taken the place of her husband, fulfilling His promise to be a husband to the widows and a father to the orphans.

She followed the path of self-denial taken by the holy fathers, who remained humble, despite the mighty wonders the Lord performed in their lives, using their humility as a shield against the enemy's snares. Thus, the Lord magnified His works in this widow's life, helping her raise her children in the fear of God and allowing her to complete her days in His favor.

CHAPTER TEN

The Blessing of the Lord Makes One Rich, and He Adds No Sorrow with It

I t is widely known that wealth often brings with it troubles and difficulties. The trials of the rich are many— temptation, pride, reliance on money, and, ultimately, the love of money, which is the root of all kinds of evil (1 Tim 6:10).

However, let no one think that money itself is inherently evil. The Lord has always preserved for Himself witnesses to His love from every class of humanity. Many wealthy individuals in every generation glorified God in their lives, and their abundance did not lead them away from the true Source of riches. On the contrary, their many talents became a cause for salvation, as they invested their resources and reaped far greater treasures, leaving behind a fragrant memory in the history of the Church.

A Living Example

Abu Bushra started his life in extreme poverty, residing with his wife and children in a simple room that resembled a shack more than a home.[8] This shelter often failed to protect them from the heavy rain of Alexandria, despite the repairs the poor man tried to make with his limited resources. On winter nights, rain would seep through, adding to their suffering from the cold, as they lacked adequate clothing and sources of warmth.

In his early years, during the 1930s, Abu Bushra worked as a traveling seller of grains. He would rent a small cart, put lentils, rice, beans, and other goods on it, and wander the streets and alleys of Gheit El-Enab and Gherbal in Alexandria, pulling his cart by hand. At the end of each day, he would earn only a few coins from this simple trade.

Great Contentment

In his extreme poverty, this modest man demonstrated one of the most vital truths of life: joy, contentment, and inner peace do not come from material possessions. Abu Bushra's life was full of rejoicing. He was content with his simple lifestyle and radiated joy to everyone around him. He was saintly in all his simple dealings with the women who bought grains from him,

---

[8] *Abu* (أبو) is an Arabic term meaning 'father of' and is often used as a form of respectful address or a nickname. It is usually followed by the name of the person's eldest child or a characteristic of the person.

thanked God in every circumstance, prayed constantly, and regularly attended the Divine Liturgy with his wife and children.

Giving out of Poverty

Some of Abu Bushra's greatest virtues were his love for the poor and his spirit of generosity. No one could imagine that a poor man like him could give anything, as people tend to give only from their surplus. However, when grace dwells in a person, it transforms even poverty into a source of wealth and abundance. Abu Bushra's humble heart became a dwelling place for grace, fulfilling the saying, "poor, yet making many rich" (2 Cor 6:10). He was diligent in giving a tithe of the few coins he earned each day, offering it to widows and those even poorer than himself. He did so joyfully and secretly, ensuring his acts of kindness would not be known, lest he lose his heavenly reward (Mt 6:4).

He Lifts up the Humble

The Lord willed to lift up His humble servant and make him a glorious example before many souls—like an icon placed upon a lampstand for all who enter to see its light (Mt 5:15). The grace of God blessed his small trade, causing it to grow at an astonishing rate. God continued to bless Abu Bushra abundantly, and he rented a small shop. Yet through all this, he remained faithful—faithful in his life, faithful in his principles, and faithful before his God. His love for serving the poor only increased with time.

Give to Whoever Asks

All the people of the neighborhood testified that this man fulfilled the words of the Lord Jesus to the letter. No beggar ever entered his shop and left empty-handed. The neighborhood was poor, and the needs of its people were endless. Yet, his heart was open to all.

He never asked anyone requesting assistance what their name was, what religion they professed, or the extent of their need. He never refused anyone's request or caused anyone to lose hope.

All day long, poor children would say things like, "Please give me an onion, Amm Abu Bushra!" or "Please give me some rice, Amm Abu Bushra!" He never sent anyone away; he blessed everyone with a generous smile and gave without counting.

The more he gave, the more grace was poured upon him in abundance, until he became very wealthy and one of the largest merchants in the neighborhood. Yet, his original simplicity remained, and he only grew in thanksgiving and generosity.

With Fr. Bishoy Kamel

Abu Bushra usually attended St. Mark Church, and he loved it with all his heart. He had a deep liking for St. Mark the Evangelist, and he always entered the church with great reverence and piety. On many occasions, Fr. Bishoy and I would encounter him at St. Mark Church or at the Patriarchate, and he would greet us with immense joy and affection.

I once heard him say to Fr. Bishoy, with tears filling his eyes, "Father, you know me well. I am a poor man who used to live happily. In the past, I lived a simple and happy life, earning five or six piasters, which were just what I needed, as I could manage them and sleep easy. Today, I have a great responsibility that I cannot bear. Why did the Lord give me all this wealth? I do not know how to handle it properly. Please, Father, pray for me."

The man wept as though bearing the weight of many sins. My heart broke at the sight of this holy man, whom I knew gave to the Lord with a generosity rarely found in this generation.

After expressing these thoughts, he completely emptied his wallet into the hands of Fr. Bishoy, insisting that Fr. Bishoy pray that God may forgive any shortcomings in his giving. And so, the Lord continued to be wonderfully generous to him.

Another Story

One day, Fr. Bishoy went to Abu Bushra's shop to buy beans for the poor, as it was a fasting season. During the short time he stood there, he noticed that more than 15 poor people came in to ask for something. Not a single one of them was turned away empty-handed. Nor did Abu Bushra ask anyone for their name.

This sight filled Fr. Bishoy with admiration. He asked Abu Bushra, "Do you give to everyone who asks, or only to those who are truly in need?"

With confidence and joy, Abu Bushra replied, "Only those who are in need."

Fr. Bishoy, surprised at this response, then asked, "How do you know they are in need? Do you know them personally?"

Abu Bushra shook his head and said, "No, but I know one thing for sure: every morning, I ask our Lord Jesus Christ to bless my day and to send me only those who are truly in need—and to keep away those who deceive. He is responsible for these people. If He has sent them to me, then they must all be in need. There is no reason for me to ask them."

Fr. Bishoy left the shop glorifying God, who has preserved such faithful people.

In Times of Crisis

At the end of the 1960s, there were frequent crises in food supply, especially during fasting seasons. There was an increase in the prices of beans, lentils, and similar items, and some of these products disappeared entirely from the markets. Even the wealthy barely managed to obtain these goods, paying unusually high prices for that time. It was during the Great Fast when Abu Bushra met us at St. Mark Church and asked, "Do you have any beans or lentils?" Before we could respond, he said, "Christ helps me and sends me food for my poor brethren to fast with." In the evening, a truck stopped in front of the church. It was loaded with more than 40 bags of beans and lentils. Abu Bushra did this for many other churches.

With his humble and spiritual conduct, he encouraged many to walk the path of generosity. He was an example of self-denial, never seeking praise from others nor wishing his name to appear on donation receipts, the sanctuary curtain, or any seat in the church. He fulfilled the Lord's commandments, so that he might obtain a full reward in the kingdom of heaven.

After raising his children in the fear of God and completing his days in a life pleasing to Christ, he joined the ranks of the righteous. Now, because of his holy life, filled with liturgies, pure sacrifices, acts of mercy, and gifts that were a sweet-smelling aroma to the Lord, he shines eternally in heaven, enjoying the reward of the saints.

CHAPTER ELEVEN

Fruit According to Its Kind

A tree is known by its fruit; "You will know them by their fruits. Do men gather grapes from thornbushes or figs from thistles? Even so, every good tree bears good fruit, but a bad tree bears bad fruit" (Mt 7:16–17). Heaven and earth will pass away, but these words will not pass away (Mt 24:35). They are proven every day in our lives and in the lives of those close to us.

This man was a well-known doctor at an urban center in Upper Egypt. His heart was filled with the fear of the Lord, and he followed Christ's commandments faithfully. I saw him every summer at St. George Church in Sporting, Alexandria. He would frequently attend church with great devotion and piety, and he partook of the Holy Sacraments regularly. I felt great shame when this man, advanced in years, stood before me confessing with tears in his eyes. In my heart, I felt small before him.

Since I only saw him a few times each summer, I knew little about him beyond what he shared in confession or brief conversations after the Divine Liturgy. At one point, years passed without sight of him. Then, one summer day, I found him standing before me in the northern altar. I was overjoyed and began asking about his well-being. He told me that his wife had departed, and he now lived alone, dedicating all his time to prayer and meditation on the word of life. Though his health had declined, he radiated an inner peace that gave his old age an air of grace and dignity.

He requested that he speak to me in greater detail about a problem he was facing. So, when the liturgy ended and everyone left, we sat in a quiet corner of the church, and I asked him what was troubling him.

He said, "I have been thinking of freeing my mind from everything that preoccupies me. I want to live these remaining days free from all burdens. So, I decided to get my finances in order, especially with my children, to avoid leaving them in confusion or leaving anything unresolved. I want to be at peace."

I said, "This would be a good thing to do. So, what is the problem then?"

"I have one son, who recently graduated from university, and two daughters, who are married and live in Alexandria. One is married to a doctor and the other to an engineer. I thank my God that they are both successful in their lives, are well-off, and have no need for anything. As for me, the Lord has granted me some of this fleeting world's possessions—a few acres of land and two buildings. I wanted to divide these among my children while I am still alive. When I spoke with my son about this, he was deeply affected, shed many tears, and refused my decision. But I insisted, explaining that this would bring me peace, joy, and contentment, as I no longer need anything. After much discussion, he reluctantly agreed, but only under the condition that his share would not exceed that of either of his sisters. I was overjoyed by his spirit, full of love, and his detachment from the world, even at such a young age.

"Then, I traveled to Alexandria and visited my eldest daughter. I spoke with her about my decision, but she firmly refused. I spent hours pleading with her, asking her to accept this for my peace of mind and inner rest. Finally, she agreed. However, when I conveyed her brother's wish to divide everything equally among them, she became upset, wept profusely, and pleaded with me, saying, 'I lack nothing. God's grace in my home is more than sufficient. My brother is young, just starting his life; you should give him everything. If I must take something, let it be a small blessing to ease your mind.'"

I looked at the man, greatly intrigued, and asked what happened next.

He continued, "The most surprising stance was that of my younger daughter, who outright refused to accept anything.

She even threatened to cut ties with me if I proceeded with such a decision."

I said, "This is indeed a strange argument."

"Please come with me to my daughters and help me convince them. I do not want them to live in discord. I have always taught them to live in peace with God and with one another."

I went with the man to witness this wonderful fruit of a genuine spiritual life. Before departing from this world, he saw with his own eyes the fruit of the spiritual life he had lived: the sweet principles he had instilled in his children. Their souls were like those in Paradise, trampling down on greed, selfishness, and the vanities of the world.

The story of this righteous man and his children brought to mind for me the early Church, which steadfastly avoided worldly gain and adhered to these teachings of the Holy Bible: "Let each of us please his neighbor for his good, leading to edification" (Rom 15:2), "Be kindly affectionate to one another with brotherly love, in honor giving preference to one another" (Rom 12:10), and "It is more blessed to give than to receive" (Acts 20:35). I felt great sorrow reflecting on the circumstances we face every day—problems of greed, the insatiable desire for more, selfishness, enmities, bitter court disputes over inheritances, and countless forms of hatred and evil. How I wished to see more of this man's example lived out in my lifetime! But such fruit does not appear by chance.

As the Lord declared, every tree bears fruit according to its kind (Gen 1:11).

CHAPTER TWELVE

Deacon Youssef Habib

D eacon Youssef Habib was a rare example of dedication. He had pure intentions to please and love Jesus alone, with no earthly goals or expectations of rewards. He wholeheartedly refused earthly rewards—praise, positions, titles, appearances, attire, ranks, money, authority, or anything of the like. This is how Deacon Youssef Habib, a true ascetic, lived until the last day of his sojourning on earth.

From his early youth, he was a servant and deacon in the Church of the Virgin Mary in Moharram Bek, Alexandria. Although he was older than the servants of the generation led by Fr. Bishoy Kamel in this church, his youthful spirit coincided with the younger servants, who were full of spiritual zeal, and he was closely connected to them.

Beginning of Consecration

The Lord of the Vineyard called His chosen one, Fr. Bishoy, to be ordained as a priest and shepherd in early December 1959. Deacon Youssef, who was then a senior officer at the Alexandria Traffic Department, attended the liturgy and ordination. It was a significant turning point in his life. He was stirred with holy zeal and said to himself, "Young men are dedicating themselves to Christ out of love for Him, joyfully offering their youth to the One who died for them, and here I am, lazy and negligent to this extent!"

That same day, Deacon Youssef went to work and presented his resignation. He then consecrated his time, effort, and entire life to a greater purpose.

His Life in Consecration

Deacon Youssef was a man of the church of rare caliber. When the newly ordained Fr. Bishoy returned to Alexandria after spending 40 days in the Monastery of St. Mary El-Sourian, he found Deacon Youssef completely devoted, day and night, to the service of the new Church of St. George in Sporting. Deacon Youssef had taken it upon himself to support Fr. Bishoy at the beginning of his priesthood.

At that time, the church, in its infancy, lacked servants, deacons, and a cantor. El-Mekaddes Youssef became the cantor, learning by heart everything that was chanted and spoken during church services and reciting it all perfectly with a touching voice and prayerful spirit.[9] He also gave himself to the service of the church's youth, watering these little seeds with care. He helped them drink from the spirit of the fathers and raised them in the love of the Church, its sacraments, and its hymns. This went on until the Church of St. George settled down and came to have its own choir of deacons, as well as a cantor. He then faded himself out in astonishing humility and self-denial to find a new area of service where he could continue to keep the Church traditions alive.

The Lives of the Saints

Deacon Youssef was fascinated by the lives of the saints, particularly those whose lives had not been made public. He began to tour monasteries, seeking the treasures that were hidden within them. He also bought a train ticket to Cairo twice a week to visit libraries, particularly the Patriarchate Library, and the Coptic Museum.

He translated and compiled the lives of the saints and the sayings of the holy fathers into small booklets that were beneficial for service and edification. This brought to light hundreds of biographies and rare stories that would encourage many generations to repent and live with God. In his great asceticism, this man cheerfully spent his entire pension on

---

[9] *El-Mekaddes* (المقدس) is an Arabic title meaning "holy man." During this period, it was typically given to individuals who had visited the Holy Land.

these matters. He did not save anything for himself, nor did any of the numerous books he published bring him any financial return. Rather, he lived as a poor man, owning absolutely nothing. He was a hermit and an ascetic in his appearance, his food and drink, and his clothing, until the day of his departure.

Fleeing from Recognition

The books multiplied and spread throughout the churches in Egypt. They were the firstfruits of a holy endeavor.

Word of the books even reached the ears of Pope Kyrillos VI. One day, Fr. Bishoy and I were visiting the pope, and he said to Fr. Bishoy, "My son, why don't you send us this Youssef Habib? He would be useful here, and he can stay with us."

Fr. Bishoy went back to Alexandria and, with wisdom and calmness, told Deacon Youssef, "His Holiness the pope asked about you and wishes to see you."

Surprised, he asked, "Why would he want to see me?"

Fr. Bishoy assured him that there was nothing wrong and said, "He may want to give you a better opportunity to read and study in the Patriarchate Library."

Fr. Bishoy and I agreed that, on our next visit to the Patriarchate in Cairo, Deacon Youssef would accompany us. And so, the next time we went to Cairo as part of the Council of the Priests of Alexandria to meet the pope, he came along. When we got there, only the priests were allowed to enter first, and Deacon Youssef waited outside.

After the meeting, Fr. Bishoy and I stayed behind, and the pope asked about Youssef Habib. We told him that he was waiting outside, and he said, "Let him come in."

We went out to call him but found no one outside. When we asked the people who were in the room with him, they said that he left as soon as the fathers entered the meeting. We looked for him in the church and the library, but we could not find him. We went back to the pope and told him that Deacon Youssef had run away, to which he replied, "Whoever knowingly runs away from an honor will be pursued by it."

When we got back to Alexandria, we met Deacon Youssef and asked where he had been.

He answered, "I asked myself, what would the pope want with a wretched man like me? I ran out of the Patriarchate. The Lord saved me."

Deacon Youssef was a humble man, desiring no honor. He would always say, "It is better for a person to remain small."

The Church of St. Takla Haymanot

At the end of the 1960s, the Lord gave us the opportunity to begin working on the new Church of St. Takla Haymanot in Ibrahimia, Alexandria.

Once again, a feeling of responsibility overtook Deacon Youssef. Without hesitation, he dedicated himself to service. With a spirit of vigilance, dedication, and self-denial, he served as the cantor and deacon in every liturgy and Vespers prayer, for the Lord had blessed him with many gifts.

One day, when the church was still in its early stages, we were offering the morning incense and were met with a problem. Because the reading books were not yet fully available, we would typically read the passages directly from the Bible, but when it came time to read the Gospel that day, we could not find an Arabic Bible. With great simplicity, Deacon Youssef picked up the Katameros and opened that day's chapter.[10] He stood reading the Gospel to the congregation, translating it from Coptic to Arabic instantaneously.

Deacon Youssef was fluent in both Bohairic and Sahidic Coptic. By translating many manuscripts into Arabic, he brought to light the valuable teachings from these treasures.

---

[10] The *Katameros* is the Coptic Orthodox Church's lectionary, containing daily Scripture readings from the Old Testament, Psalms, Epistles, and Gospels, structured according to the liturgical calendar.

His Love for Young People

He once told me, "When a sinful young man comes to you, know without a doubt that he has been sent to you by the Lord Himself. It is as if he carries a recommendation letter from Jesus Christ, personally saying, 'I ask you to care for him for the sake of My wounds and My spilled blood, and I will reward you for your kindness.' You must receive him with compassion and love and tend to his needs."

The Angel of the Altar

Another time, he told me, "You must make friends with the angel of the altar and make sure he approves of you, particularly when you go around the altar. If he approves of you, he will walk with you as you pass through the congregation. He will hold you with his right hand as you go around with the incense, and your voice will be heard and kept in the hearts of the congregation. He will follow your footsteps in every good deed, heal all your bodily illnesses, and make you strong in prayer. But if the priest is not pleasing to the angel, the angel of the altar will part from him, and he will lose his dignity and become powerless, in a state of forsakenness."

I was greatly surprised and asked him if this was according to the sayings of the saintly fathers.

He said, "Isn't the angel of the altar, whom you serve, the one who lifts prayers and sacrifices of praise to heaven?"

Wisdom in His Silence

Deacon Youssef's approach to public issues and church disputes showed true sincerity and humility. Everyone who knew him said that he considered himself too small to deal with such matters, which only concerned elders. No one could recall Deacon Youssef ever participating in controversial discussions on any subject concerning the church or its leaders.

One time, he said to me, "Do you know why the wise St. Arsenius was silent?"

He then explained, "The Church, at that time, was overcome with great controversies over Origen. Some passionately supported and defended him, while others opposed him and his conduct and considered him excommunicated from the Church. St. Arsenius refused to be drawn into fruitless discussions. He didn't receive visitors, nor did he speak to anyone, preferring to remain silent. He turned his silence into prayer and life with God. He loved all people by staying away from all."

I later learned that Deacon Youssef had published a book about St. Arsenius and that he grew close to this saint, following his spiritual path by rising above circumstances and loving all people without argument or division.

A Wish Granted

Deacon Youssef lived alone and handled every aspect of his life, including his food, clothing, and appearance, with great humility. He lived on very little.

He always said that his greatest request from Christ was that he would remain on his feet until the day of his departure. He said, "I do not want to be sick and trouble anyone with taking care of me. The very fact that I can walk on my feet is the greatest gift."

The Lord granted His faithful servant this wish. He did not get sick, so people did not have to care for him. When his time came, Christ peacefully relieved him of the troubles of the world.

CHAPTER THIRTEEN

George of Rome

After her husband departed and left her with seven children, she became one of the widows fully supported by the church. Her body was frail, and her eyesight was weak. She was unable to read or write. She prayed constantly and wept frequently, holding on to the Lord's promise that He is "A father of the fatherless, a defender of widows" (Ps 68:5).

She made great efforts to educate her children, and the Lord held her hand in miraculous ways. One day, she came to the church asking about someone who had given her exceptional help.

She insisted on seeing him, saying to a deacon, "Please tell me where I can find George."

The deacon replied, "George who?"

She said, with great certainty, "George of Rome."

The deacon asked, "Where does he live?"

She replied, "He told me he lives here in the church."

I happened to enter the church at this time, and I heard the deacon say, "I know nothing about him. Fr. Louka is here, and you can ask him."

I asked her what was going on, and she began to tell me a story that was beyond imagination.

"My daughter scored poorly on her preparatory school exams this year and wasn't accepted into public secondary schools. I have been struggling with her, running around, visiting many schools. Finally, I went to a private commercial secondary school yesterday and met the principal and teachers. They told me the first installment was 18 pounds. I only had eight pounds, which I had received from the church. I begged them, cried, and asked them to accept her papers and take the eight pounds, but they refused. I left the school in tears, and, as I stepped out, I looked up to the sky and said, 'Lord, You are the father of orphans and the defender of widows. There is nothing I can do.' After I had walked a few steps, I heard someone calling out to me gently, and I was scared. I hid my purse close to my chest, fearing someone might snatch it. I was too scared to look back, but the voice calling me came closer. When I turned around, I found a man whose face shone with great radiance and dignity. He had a majestic appearance. He said to me, 'Wipe your tears first. What do you need?' I said, 'I want my daughter to be accepted into school.' He said, 'Come with me.'"

She continued, "We got into a big car, went to the educational district, and entered a large building full of employees. He took me to the director of secondary education and gave him my daughter's file. He then took me back to the car and, without asking for my address, dropped me off near my home. He said, 'In three days, you will receive a yellow card in the mail. This will be the letter of your daughter's acceptance into the government secondary commercial school.' I prayed for his long life and insisted he come home with me so I could host him, but he thanked me and declined. I asked him his name, and he told me, 'I am George of Rome.' When I asked where he lived, he said, 'I am always at the Church of St. George in Sporting.'"

Everything happened exactly as he said. Her daughter was admitted to the secondary commercial school. The headmistress took great care of her daughter, as though she had been specially recommended. I could hardly believe my ears as the woman was telling me this.

She said, "Please, do me a favor. Let me see this man, so that I may kiss his hands and thank him."

I said to her, "Describe him to me once again."

"I cannot see very well, but he was fair-skinned with blue eyes, and he looked like a prince."

I said, "He is always here at every liturgy and Vespers prayer, standing in the church. If you come during the prayers, you will find him. But don't stare at everyone. He is always in the last row of the church, guarding his children."

I was sure that this was the work of the great St. George of Rome. He appeared to this poor widow, who had no helper in the world. I glorified God, who gives power to His people and sends His saints to aid those who hope in Him and call upon His name.

CHAPTER FOURTEEN

Let Me Die the Death of the Righteous

One of the most unusual departure stories I've ever heard is that of the holy Beshara El-Kassis, brother of the blessed Pope Macarius III and father of both His Eminence Abba Athanasius, Metropolitan of Beni Suef, and the late Fr. Mikhail Beshara, priest of St. George Church in El-Mahalla El-Kubra.

Fr. Mikhail himself recounted the story to me in the presence of several of his relatives, all of whom were eyewitnesses of the final moments of Amm Beshara's life.

Throughout his lifetime, Amm Beshara was known by all as a virtuous and saintly man, one who feared God and loved Him with all his heart. The Lord's blessings rested upon his home and children. Amm Beshara was respected by his family, his neighbors, and outsiders, too. He was well-known for his love for everyone, his hospitality, and his great care for strangers and travelers.

One day, as he sat by the door of his house, a group of young men passed by. He invited them in, as it was his custom to welcome everyone and offer a meal to every visitor. When the young men were seated, he rose like Abraham (Gen 18:1–8), the father of the patriarchs, and asked his wife to prepare food for the guests, even though they were strangers to him.

She apologized, saying she had no bread to offer because she had not yet baked that day. Only a few scraps remained in the breadbasket. He told her to offer what they had, trusting that the Lord would bless it.

The young men overheard the conversation between the man and his wife and decided to take the opportunity to embarrass him. They agreed to finish all the food he offered and then ask for more.

Amm Beshara came out with the scraps of bread and some cheese, placed them before the group, and, as was his custom, blessed the food with the sign of the cross. They began to eat with great appetites, intending to consume everything, but, strangely, the food would not run out. They ate until they were completely full and could eat no more; this went on until they felt sick from overeating.

Then, they said, "Amm Beshara, please tell us the spell you used to keep the food from running out."

In this manner, the hand of God was with Amm Beshara and His blessings fell on him.

His Death

Fr. Mikhail was staying with Amm Beshara on the day of his passing. Although he appeared to be in normal health, at midnight, he awoke and asked those present to wake Fr. Mikhail because he was about to depart to the Lord. Everyone was surprised and tried to avoid disturbing Fr. Mikhail, especially since Amm Beshara seemed completely healthy and had just come out of the bathroom walking on his own feet.

When they finally woke Fr. Mikhail, he hurried in to check on his father, but Amm Beshara assured him he was fine. He got into his bed on his own and began offering spiritual advice to Fr. Mikhail regarding service, praises, the congregation, and love toward his brothers and sisters—advice that was thoroughly Christian. He then asked Fr. Mikhail to read him the absolution. Fr. Mikhail, deeply disturbed and troubled, reluctantly complied.

While reading, Fr. Mikhail stumbled over his words, so the man opened his eyes and said, "Read the absolution properly."

As Fr. Mikhail continued reading, the man closed his eyes, and the women present began to cry out. He opened his eyes again and said, "Why this commotion and crying? Pray instead." He then began assigning each of them a psalm to recite. Afterward, he asked Fr. Mikhail to finish reading the absolution.

The moment Fr. Mikhail concluded, the righteous man gave up his spirit into the hands of God with the peace and tranquility of the saints. More than 10 people were present to witness this spiritual scene at the man's bedside, which the angels surrounded with great respect. When he departed, the women began to weep, but Fr. Mikhail stopped them, asking them to complete their prayers and psalms, which the blessed Beshara had begun with them.

CHAPTER FIFTEEN

Jesus, Helper of the Afflicted

In every generation, the Lord chooses people to whom He gives abundant wisdom and insight. The Lord gave our sister Fawzeya Ishak an unusual purity of heart and a unique perception that unveiled strange matters.

She would see visions from God and know of momentous events before they would happen. For example, at dawn on Tuesday, March 9, 1971, she woke her husband, Dr. Onsi, in great distress and said to him, "What a great loss, my dear. Pope Kyrillos has departed to heaven."

He asked her, "How did you know that?"

She replied, "My departed sister Julia just came to me and said, 'We have descended in a great procession from above to take Pope Kyrillos with us, so he can be with us in the place where we are.'"

Pope Kyrillos VI departed to heaven a few hours after this vision. At the time, she was living in Luxor, hundreds of miles away from the pope's residence in Cairo.

A Strange Revelation

Similarly, when she was living in Luxor and her father was living in Alexandria, she woke up in the middle of the night and said to her husband, "Dad has departed and is now at rest from his sufferings. I just saw him being carried by angels ascending to heaven."

They received the news of his death the next morning. When they got to Alexandria, they learned that the time of his departure was precisely the hour she had seen him ascending to heaven in her vision.

A Procession of Angels

She was a wife and mother with a serene soul and a pure heart; she did not care for the vanities and deceptions of the world and lived a simple life of contentment. Later in her life, the Lord allowed her to undergo the trial of illness; she suffered from cancer.

In the last two years of her life, she endured pain beyond measure. Yet, her portion of comfort from the Lord far exceeded the pain, fulfilling the words of the apostle, "For our light affliction, which is but for a moment, is working for us a far more exceeding and eternal weight of glory" (2 Cor 4:17).

Agreement on the Time of Her Departure

The manner in which the Lord appointed the time of her departure was unimaginably strange. On January 4, 1984, when she was burdened by great pain, she called her husband early in the morning and said, "Come here, dear. I have something to tell you, and please don't be upset. Last night, I was with Christ, and He said to me, 'That's enough—you've taken all your sufferings, and your crown is ready. If you'd like to come to Me now, I am ready for you.' But I told Him, 'Forgive me, Jesus. Though the pain is unbearable without Your support, I love my children very much. I'm willing to bear it for their sake until they celebrate Christmas and Epiphany and enjoy their time with their friends at church during the mid-year break. I'll come to You on the last day of their break, Friday, January 27, so they can start their studies again the next day.' Jesus agreed with me and promised to fulfill my wish. So, I'll go to heaven on Friday, the last day of the mid-year break. Are you okay with that, or are you upset, dear?"

Her husband composed himself and, with great effort, replied, "How could I object to something Jesus has approved? Let His will be done."

The Lord indeed fulfilled His promise. He released her from the prison of her body in peace on Friday, January 27, at the exact hour she had agreed upon with her Beloved.

What a marvel—this woman had intimacy and agreement with her Lord to this extent! How wondrous is Your name, O Lord, how wondrous is Your love, and how wondrous is the glory You have prepared for Your saints! The Lord often comforts His saints by revealing to them the times of their departures days in advance. However, I had never heard of anything quite like this.

Her husband documented her visions, her profound, heartfelt advice, and excerpts from her prayers, believing them to be invaluable for every soul. May her example be a source of comfort to all those suffering and a reminder of the better life, imperishable crown, and inheritance reserved for us in heaven.

Stories of Her Holiness

Dr. Onsi told us about the grace that supported his wife's faith until the end and the boldness that helped her attain her great degree of love, which allowed for agreement between her and God. He shared with us some of his wife's visions, revelations, fervent prayers, and precious advice that he recorded. These can be valuable to every soul.

Due to the constant, intense pain that prevented her from experiencing restful sleep, she would often drift into a light slumber, aided by sedatives and painkillers. One time, she was lying half asleep, and, dozing off, she began to speak simple, clear, and profound words that expressed her emotions, meditations, and advice. She also spoke about the revelations of spiritual and heavenly visions she experienced while in the grip of severe pain.

Some of these revelations confirm that she had encounters with the Lord Jesus, the Beloved of our souls, who, in His love, appeared to her many times, revealing Himself and surrounding her with His light and beauty. He had conversations with her, through which He provided her with hope, comfort, and reassurance. He alleviated her pain, so that she not only endured it or patiently bore it, but also thanked Him for it and rejoiced in it.

Dr. Onsi recounted some of what she said during the final months of her period of suffering.

He said, "My beloved wife—may God rest her soul—would speak these words clearly and simply. She was not addressing any of us in particular; she spontaneously expressed her feelings and deepest emotions. Although she spoke while in great pain, her words were coherent, clear, simple, deep, and purposeful. As I listened to her alone during the night, I felt that these words were coming from a heart filled with God's complete peace. It was as though the gentle, kind spirit within her prompted her to utter words of firm wisdom. Truly, they were words of the Spirit spoken through a heart broken by the harshness of pain yet filled with God's presence and the Holy Spirit, as well as the comfort, joy, and peace that comes with Him."

He went on, "One night, I heard her say, 'Jesus Christ, You alone can satisfy us. We will never find satisfaction in our bodies, no matter how much we eat, dress, or acquire. Look at me now—my body withers away day by day, and even a small morsel of food gets stuck in my throat. I thank You for showing me that You are my satisfaction because I see You next to me in my deepest pain. When I was well, I could not see You. This is why, now, I am patient, thankful, and joyful. If only people would make room for You in their lives. The devil deceives them into filling their hearts with worldly matters until there is no place left for You. I beg You, my Lord, give everyone true happiness in Your presence. Help them to make space for You in their hearts and minds, so they can experience true joy—a joy that not even the greatest pains can shake. Even amidst my intense pain, which I can't fully describe, You have given me grace. In my great sufferings, I see Your great gifts to me, which I know I don't deserve. I rejoice, remain patient, and affirm that, just as I have received the good things, I must thankfully accept what is bitter from Your hands. Even the bitter things are great gifts because I see them as tiny fragments of the cross, allowing me to share in Your suffering. When I see people, particularly my beloved believers, trying to find satisfaction in worldly endeavors, it grieves me deeply—like when they look at shop windows and think they will find happiness there. Let them know. Show them, my Lord, that You are the living source of joy, love, and richness—that their fountain of life is You, the loving and bountiful God, who always loves to give. The more You see us rejoicing in Your love, the more You give to us. A life with You, Lord, is the ultimate success. You were with Joseph, and the Bible says he succeeded in all things. Please, Lord, let my children live for You and in You, that they may live the life of true joy in purity, faithfulness, humility, meekness, and contentment. Preserve their lives in Your love, that they may love one another and love all people, even the evil ones, for Your sake. May they pray for them also, for the sake of Your cross, which has redeemed all.'

"She continued, 'I thank You, my Lord Jesus, for this affliction has shown me Your beauty that surpasses all human beauty. I have seen much, and You have given me much. I have had great happiness, but it was all limited and fleeting. My joy in You is always increasing and eternal. Without this joy, I could not have survived a single moment of my intense suffering, which I have endured every moment of throughout these long months. I am joyful in You and in the garment of glory I have seen prepared for me. You told me I will wear it soon.'

"'My dear children, I also want you to always rejoice because life with Jesus is a life of continuous joy. After I leave you, rejoice because I will have put on the garment of glory and light and cast off the garment of pain and suffering. Would you resent that your mother is being escorted to heaven? There, her spirit will be with you even more than it is here, and she will have a greater role in your lives than she does now. When my own mother departed from this world, I knelt by her bed and prayed for her and for myself, asking the Lord to grant me faith and strength. The trial passed in peace, and God helped me to always feel that she was with me and I was with her. I want you to be the same—never grieve, so I won't be saddened in my heavenly joy. And I am certain that God will be with you more and more. When I go to Him, He will be glorified even more through you, and you will have success in everything. Serve Him and serve His Church—your true mother, who gave birth to you through Baptism. Live lives of purity, so the Holy Spirit may dwell in you and remain with you. Do not be concerned with the world. Always do what is right. If people are pleased, that's good; if not, it doesn't matter. Even Christ Himself was rejected by many.'

"'I have learned much from my experience. I used to care about appearances and people's opinions. After the many lessons the Lord has given me, I found that those who were better than me have gone to the worms and dust. I realized that caring about appearances is a deception that we must not fall into. Since then, I have loved complete simplicity and the pure nature of everything, to the extent that many have criticized and insulted me because of my appearance and other matters. But nothing mattered to me as long as I pleased Christ, who, while on earth, was simple and recommended simplicity in everything—not just in appearance and clothing, but in everything, even food. All these things, my children, do not matter. It all goes to rot with the worms. Your souls are the only things you should preserve and take care of, because souls are everlasting. If we give the body more than what is necessary, it could lead to our perdition and the loss of our salvation. It is true that you should seek success in your earthly life, but do not think that worldly success is of any value if it is not accompanied by spiritual success; otherwise, it is as if it never existed. What matters most is the success of your souls, above all else. Earthly success will end and the lack of it will make no difference.'

"Then, she groaned deeply and said, 'Oh, the pain is so intense, but it's enough for me, Jesus, that I see You and that You are with me. This comforts me, brings me joy, and enables me to endure everything.'"

Dr. Onsi continued, "On another night, she again moaned from the excruciating pain, and then she dozed off after a morphine injection. A moment later, I woke up to her saying, 'What I see is really beautiful, Onsi.'

"I asked her, 'What do you see?'

"'I see Jesus. He is so beautiful that I cannot describe such beauty.'

"I answered, 'Certainly, He is the most beautiful among the sons of men,' and she said, 'Indeed, indeed.'

"I asked, 'Did He say anything to you?'

"'Yes. He said, 'Would you like to come now?' and I said, 'Yes, of course, I am longing to come, but in a little while. Let me talk to my children and advise again that they hold on to You. Then, it will be over, and I will come to You.'"

"She moaned again and said, 'Oh! The pain is very severe, but I thank You, Jesus, because You are with me, and You strengthen me. I do not deserve all Your gifts. You humble me with them. I do not even deserve the injection that relieves the pain, and which is not available to everybody. I thank You a thousand times because I am content with Your presence. I do not feel void of anything. I wish all people would have true contentment in Christ, who is the Bread of Life. I wish all those I love would experience contentment in Him only. They would never want, fear, or hunger for anything. Once again, my children, I bid you to live happily in Christ always. Be happy for me when I am with Him in heaven until we are all together with Him there.'

"She used to speak to each of her children individually, God rest her soul, telling them the same principles and concepts, perhaps with more depth than when she spoke in her sleep. It was very important to her to establish these concepts in their hearts, that they may be firmly rooted there all their lives.

"On another night, while she was in a state between slumber and consciousness after receiving injections and sleeping pills, she said, 'I am happy with Him today and with the graces that I experienced today! The pain was most severe, and, as you know, I have received many injections, but today, Christ surrounded me and made me happy with His presence to make up for my pain. My happiness is in Him. What good have I done to make me worthy of seeing all this grace with my eyes while still alive? I don't know how to thank Him; no matter how much I thank Him, it will never be enough. Today, there is more pain, but there is also more love. This is why I rejoice in my pain. He supports me and comforts me with His two hands. These are indescribable mercies. I thank God, truly!'

"It seems that Christ—glory be to Him—never left her, night or day. In fact, I am sure that He took her at times out of her body, out of the world, to give her periods of rest, happiness, and comfort, in the same manner He took Paul the Apostle to the third heaven after he was stoned in Lystra and almost died in order to strengthen and comfort him. I was assured of this through her own words.

"One morning, we woke up and found that our beloved had departed to a strange state; she was neither asleep nor awake. As we stood bewildered, trying to figure out what this was, Dr. Mofida Moawad came to visit us. She was a devoted friend who visited my wife three times a week, and my wife always felt at ease in her presence, whether in times of joy or sorrow. She examined her, also perplexed. This state was not a coma in its usual form, nor was it death. Dr. Mofida tried to revive her by various means. After about half an hour, she suddenly opened her eyes, and Dr. Mofida asked her, 'What happened? Where were you and what is it that happened to you?' She replied, 'You have just interrupted the happiest moment of my life.' But she did not describe anything more.

However, the following night, I woke up when I heard her speaking in a clear voice.

"She said, 'This past day was very strange. It began with a great sense of rest, completely free from pain. This was the first time I had spent hours without pain in many months. I was completely happy. It was a new type of happiness that cannot be described. I saw Jesus early in the morning, and He said, 'You are one of My beloved daughters, for whom I have prepared a bigger crown. Those who truly love Me bear with Me and accept anything from Me.' I felt that I was completely healed. I actually left the world for a few moments. I do not know how long this lasted and cannot describe it. I felt that all my pains and sufferings were taken away, so that I may wear my white garments of heaven. I was extremely happy. Then, Dr. Mofida came in, and I told her that she interrupted the happiest moment of my life. The doctor thought that I was in a coma. Not at all—I was passing through life and the world, and Jesus showed me the beauty of passing, so that I may be reassured at the time of my passage, which is near.'

"Later, she repeated the same things. She told me, when she was awake in the daytime, 'I truly thank God, because the thing I was afraid of was the moment of death. But see, Onsi, how the lovingkindness of Christ freed me from my body and made me pass through the world and through life? He assured me that the hour of passing is an hour of joy and release towards Christ. I am no longer afraid because I have seen how beautiful it is!'

"She always spoke with Christ and saw His beauty and light. One night, as she was speaking to Him in her sleep, I said to her, 'I would like for you to always remember us when you are with Jesus, so that He may help us, strengthen us, and grant us mercy.'

"She replied, 'Of course I will mention you.'

"I said, 'Is that a promise?'

"'It is certainly a promise. I will have no other work to do when I am with Him there.'

"I then said, 'You will be busy with Him and with His beauty!'

"Surprised, she answered, 'Part of my busy-ness with Him will be spent remembering each of you one by one.'

"On countless nights, she expressed many thoughts about her deep life experiences with Christ, showing the beauty of fellowship with Him, the work of His grace in us, our need to hold on to Him and taste His love, as well as many other matters which we cannot deal with at length here.

"Through her words, she revealed heavenly scenes and visions of saints. One night, at about 2 a.m., she woke me up and said, 'Onsi, have no fear. Those I see outside the room can't harm us.'

"I asked her, 'Who are they?'

"She answered, 'A large group of terrifying figures— they're dark, tall, and crowded together, trying to come in. But none of them can enter because of the beautiful lady standing at the door. She assured me that she would always be there. Can you see how beautiful she is, Onsi? She is wearing a light, heavenly gown. Her face is shining, and her hands are stretched out across the door, keeping them away. I thank You, Lord, because You truly protect us.'

"Of course, the lady at the door was the mother of us all, the Virgin Mary. Now I understand what we mean when we say in the prayers of the Agpeya, 'And when my soul departs my body, attend to me, and defeat the conspiracy of the enemies, and shut the gates of Hades, lest they might swallow my soul, O you, blameless bride of the true Bridegroom' [eleventh hour litany]. Truly, my wife made us realize and understand a very important fact—that this is indeed one of the roles played by our Lady of Intercessions; in fact, it is the greatest and final role she assumes in our lives."

He continued, "One night, my wife called me, saying, 'Onsi, can you see this great light that fills the room? It is very strange. I always say that my eyes cannot tolerate electric light, even when it's dim. So, why is it that, when I look at this light, I'm happy with it? It does not exert my eyes. It is truly a strong light, but it is restful and beautiful.' Truly, this was the light of our beloved Christ, who is the Sun of Righteousness and the Light of the World!

"She always drew a parallel between the severity of her pains and what her beloved Jesus revealed to her. She used to say, 'Why do you feel bad and cry and make me sad? If I am happy with my pains and see Christ and His glory in them, why should you be sad?'

"One time, she was in such severe pain that her face was flushed, and her bed swayed, as she trembled with excruciating pain. At that time, Fr. Kyrillos Dawood was the father of the Church of Archangel Michael in Mostafa Kamel. When he saw her greatly suffering, he tearfully prayed a fervent and powerful prayer that came from the depths of his soul. After he left, she said to me, 'Do you see how every pain comes with an even greater blessing and reward? The blessings exceed the pain. If I had not experienced this pain in the presence of Fr. Kyrillos, we would have missed the blessing that we obtained from this holy prayer.' Thus, she spiritually analyzed all matters during her long and cruel illness."

These are glimpses of the overwhelming comfort that this saintly woman experienced amidst her physical suffering. She was a truly unique example of God's works and His endless mercies. Her life became a source of blessing and comfort to many who knew and loved her. The story of her fight and endurance is a message to carry the cross thankfully and joyfully. God's consolation and His true promises strengthened her faith and solidified her hope.

May her story be an encouragement to all who suffer, giving hope for a better life, an everlasting crown, and an inheritance preserved for us in heaven.

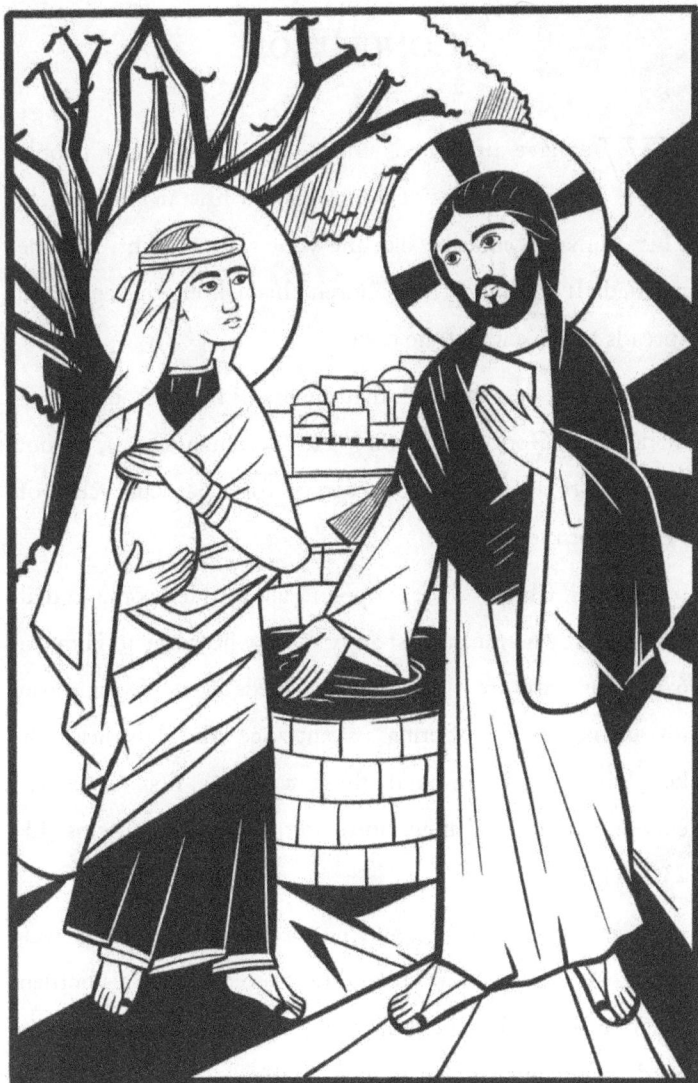

CONCLUSION

We have presented stories of ordinary holy people whose lives exude the aroma of Christ in His Church. This aroma anoints the old, the young, the virgins, and the married. It perfumes the Church throughout the ages and spreads to the ends of the earth.

You see, dear beloved, that the life of holiness, the life of being with God and keeping His commandments, is not exclusive to a select few or reserved for a particular class of people born to be saints!

Rather, Christ's door is open to all, for He promised that He would by no means cast away those who come to Him (Jn 6:37). His arms are outstretched towards us as He hangs on the cross, openly offering us entrance into His heavenly kingdom. The right-hand thief was the first to enter, encouraging us to follow, no matter how great our sins (Lk 23:42–43).

We can understand a very important truth from the lives of these just people: the yoke of Jesus is easy, and His burden is light compared to the bitter yoke of the cruel world and the deadly, merciless yoke of sin (Mt 11:30).

Let us embrace the cross and uphold the good name that calls us. Let us live a life worthy of the calling we have received

(Eph 4:1). May we abide in love, which is the first and greatest commandment (Mt 22:37–38). Let us bring joy to our Lord Jesus' heart by upholding the law of love in our everyday lives. Let there be no enmity, no wounding of the spirit of love, no judgment, no gossip, no dispute, nor any negative thing that quenches the Spirit and gives the enemy an opportunity to take advantage of us. Let us love in truth, not just with our tongues or our words, but with our works, giving abundantly of ourselves, giving dignity to others before ourselves, and sacrificing ourselves in the likeness of Christ. Let us lay down our lives for our brothers for the sake of Christ who gave Himself up for us (Jn 15:13).

Let us uphold holiness, for without it, no one can see God. Let us know how to preserve our bodies in purity of conduct and be holy as the Holy One who called us is holy. Our spirits, souls, and bodies belong to Christ. The body is not for fornication, but for God. We were bought at a precious price, the blood of Jesus Christ, the blameless Lamb. Our members now belong to Him who bought and redeemed us. Therefore, glorify God in your spirit and in your body, which belong to Him (1 Cor 6:13–20). We have become true temples of God. Whoever corrupts the temple of God, God will destroy, for the temple of God is holy (1 Cor 3:16–17).

Every day, let us put off the old man, corrupted with deceitful desires (Eph 4:22), and let us reject all former sinful behaviors through sincere repentance, tearful prayer, and pure-hearted confession. Let us put on the new man (Eph

4:24), partaking worthily and thankfully of the Eucharist, as we offer a sacrifice of praise.

May we be known for being free of the love of money and greed, for if anyone has great wealth, their life cannot be found in their possessions. May your prayers exude the aroma of joy, rising like incense from a pure heart, in complete humility, from lips that speak truth. May we enter the church and the holy places with dignity and modesty, in full consciousness and spiritual wisdom, so that we may not be condemned, like those who turned the house of the Lord into a den of thieves and saddened His heart by being diverted from Him, following their own ways (Mt 21:12–13).

Let us strive and endure patiently in the struggle through fasting and prayer. There is no despair in Christ, for He is the Savior of sinners. No power on earth can separate us from the love of Christ (Rom 8:39). Sin has no power because Christ's blood purifies us from all sins (1 Jn 1:7). Christ even overcame death and raised Lazarus after four days (Jn 11:39–44).

Let us not rely on ourselves, for many have begun in the Spirit and ended in the flesh. Christ cannot be deceived. He looks at the heart, and everything is subject to His scrutiny; "Therefore let him who thinks he stands take heed lest he fall" (1 Cor 10:12). Remember the words of our Lord Jesus Christ, "Be holy" (1 Pet 1:16).